Personhood in Advanced Old Age

Sheldon S. Tobin, PhD, received his doctorate in 1963 from the Committee on Human Development of the University of Chicago, where he remained as a faculty member of the School of Social Service Administration until 1982. He then went to the State University of New York at Albany to become Director of the Ringel Institute of Gerontology and Professor in the School of Social Welfare. He has authored over 100 publications, including six books, on adult development and aging, adaptation to stress in aging, services for the elderly, and clinical practice with the elderly. His ability to bridge the worlds of science and practice led to his appointment by the Gerontological Society of America as Editor-in-Chief, from 1985 through 1988, of *The Gerontologist*, the leading journal of applied gerontology.

Personhood in Advanced Old Age

Implications for Practice

Sheldon S. Tobin, PhD

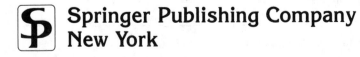

Springer Publishing Company
New York

Springer Publishing Company, Inc.
536 Broadway
New York, NY 10012-3955

91 92 93 94 95 / 5 4 3 2 1

Library of Congress Cataloging-in-Publication Date

Tobin, Sheldon S.
    Personhood in advanced old age : implications for practice /
Sheldon S. Tobin.
        p.   cm.
    Includes bibliographical references and index.
    ISBN 0-8261-7580-5
    1. Aged—Psychology. 2. Aging—Psychological aspects. 3. Aged—
Counseling of. I. Title.
    [DNLM: 1. Adaptation, Psycholigical—in old age. 2. Aged—
psychology. 3. Aging—psychology.   WT 150 T629p]
BF724.8.T63   1991
155.67—dc20
DLC   90-10444
for Library of Congress   CIP

Contents

Preface

Throughout time, some people's lives have reached the 110 years or so that is our genetic endowment. It is only in recent years, however, that large groups of people have been living into their eighties and nineties. This group, first referred to as the old-old by Neugarten (1974), is increasing at the fastest rate. With medical advances that have conquered lethal diseases, not only are people living longer, but 65 has ceased to be a significant proxy for demarcating the beginning of an old age of disability and frailty. People are indeed healthier than ever before through their later years.

Yet, concurrent with the increase in the healthy later years, the period of disability before death is lengthening. If, for example, a generation or two ago, the preterminal period of disability was from 73 to 75, by the same metric it may now be 82 to 85, that is, an increase from two to three years or so between disability and death. Moreover, if the three leading causes of death (cancer, heart disease, and stroke) were to be cured in the next decades, the average age of death for someone who lives to 65 may rise to above 90, with, however, the preterminal disability period correspondingly rising from three to more than five years. Certainly, disabilities from musculoskeletal degeneration will continue to be prevalent among the very old, as will be senile dementia. Estimates of becoming a victim of Alzheimer's disease, if one lives long enough, are very high and range from 30% to more than 50% beyond age 90.

But chronological age obscures the aging of individuals, the aging of each of us. Some of us will have many age-associated losses in our seventies, others in our eighties, and still others of us will die suddenly in our nineties having suffered minimal losses. But, for those of us who live long enough, there is likely to be a phrase toward the end of life that contains many losses. With the accumulation of losses and the waning of energies, there will probably come a time when we will begin to perceive ourselves as not only "older" or "elderly" but also as being "old."

This new self-perception of being "old" reflects a new state of mind characterized by an awareness of being irreversibly near the end of our lifespan. We shall, however, have a concomitant awareness that we are still the people we have always been, and, in turn, our desire will be to still be the same. Indeed, to preserve ourselves—our identities—will become our adaptive task, and, fortunately, most of us will be able to successfully master the task, at least in the earliest phases of oldness. Personhood, in this context refers not only to the qualities that confer distinct individuality to each person, but also to the commonalities among people of advanced old age. Some of these commonalities—the use of the past, lessened introspection, mechanisms used to facilitate adaptation to stress, and acceptance of death—have been considered by Morton A. Lieberman and me to comprise the unique psychology of the very old. Other commonalities—the experience of becoming "old," religious beliefs of being personally blessed by God in having lived a long life, and of a hereafter of reunions with deceased loved ones—have been added in constructing personhood in advanced old age. It will become apparent that whereas some elements in this personhood are adaptive for those now "old," they could be considered psychopathological when evidenced in younger persons.

In Chapter 1, on the psychology of being "old," evidence for personhood is discussed, beginning with how the stability of the self is maintained through blending the past and the present in validating the self and how the past is made vivid to reaffirm the self. Related issues are then introduced such as Erikson's (1982) reformulation of the last of his eight stages, "ego integrity versus despair," which moves him toward congruence with my formulation. Discussed next are contents of the unique psychology that are associated with adaptation to stress, particularly aggressiveness and magical coping. Case illustrations are used here and throughout the book, but, of course, pseudonyms are used and facts are altered to disguise identities. Included are the rationales for the specific usefulness of these psychological processes for the very old. Concluding the chapter is a section on well-being and then a comment on integrating qualities of personhood into practice.

Chapter 2, on applying therapeutic approaches to individuals, begins with a discussion of the clinical wisdom of practitioners who have corroborated the therapeutic usefulness of the unique psychological processes of the very old, specifically psychoanalysts who have modified their treatment for the very old who are in crises. Next discussed are the beneficial uses of the processes comprising the unique psychology, specifically mobilizing aggression, making the past vivid, and magical coping. The chapter continues with discussions of the limits of supportive psychotherapy, particularly when there is a need for action and not words; of the usefulness of reconstructive psychotherapy; and of how practitioners modify their practice with elderly individuals, extending to transference and countertransference issues. The chapter ends with a rhetorical question: So, why work with old people?

Chapter 3, on working with families, starts by detailing a family consultation session, which is then used to illustrate how psychological processes useful for preserving the self are sources of annoyance for adult offspring. Considered are complaints about aggressiveness and, specifically, paranoid accusations, the use of magical coping as reflected in attempts to do more than can be done, which may lead to harming oneself, repetitive reminiscence, and maintenance of persistent and discomforting interpersonal psychodynamics. Next comes a discussion of the typical kinds of feelings of family caregivers that are more relevant in work with families, including rage at care receivers from causing feelings of inadequacy, fears from risk-taking, frustrations associated with providers, and gratifications from caregiving. A section follows on the older care receiver, particularly on the emotional security gained from family members. The chapter ends with sections on caring for Alzheimer's disease victims, practice with elderly individuals and their families during the process of the elderly becoming institutionalized, and a final comment on who is the client in work with families.

Chapter 4 covers a topic that has received too little attention in the literature: reducing psychological distress from hospitalizations. The specific focus is on iatrogenesis, that is, deleterious effects induced inadvertently in treatment. After a brief introduction to the greater susceptibility of elderly persons to iatrogenic illness, there is a discussion of how expectations, particularly of Alzheimer's disease and depression, become self-fulfilling prophecies. A case is used to illustrate how the expectations of dementia cause hospital personnel to interpret depressed patients' inattention to their environments (a "pseudo" or false dementia) as Alzheimer's disease. To the extent that the depression is from self-blame, and that accompanying passivity is from compliance, mobilizing aggressiveness, even combativeness, can be helpful to patients. The focus then shifts to issues of patients' "autonomy," the latest *linqua franca* for patients' self-determination, and the importance of patients' feeling in control and of our promoting the kind of autonomy each patient needs to preserve an idiosyncratic self. The chapter ends with a brief comment on discharge planning.

The main message of Chapter 5, on the providing of supportive services in nursing homes, is the necessity for structuring ongoing relationships between staff and individual residents. Indeed, the usefulness of sophisticated practitioners in nursing homes is less in their one-to-one interaction with residents than with their structuring of relationships, as well as in their educating staff to the meanings of resident's behaviors and to the importance of maintaining or restoring assertiveness, of having authentic autonomy and a sense of control, of producing organized reconstructions of the past, and of preserving the self. After discussion of some of these basic principles, knowledge about the inner experiences during the process of becoming institutionalized and the predictors of adaptation will form the basis for focusing upon the necessity to enhance a sense of control. Next, working with staff to create quality environments is covered, followed by discussing behavioral approaches, and ending with a structured approach to promoting beneficial family involvement in nursing homes.

Chapter 6, on preserving the self through religion, is initiated by a discourse on the importance of religious beliefs and practices for the current cohort of the very old. Apparently, religion enhances well-being; religious coping behaviors are used to deal with difficult experiences; and cherished religious possessions aid in preserving the self. Next is a discussion on how living to old age is often associated with feeling personally blessed by God, followed by the observation that thoughts of the afterlife are of reunions with deceased loved ones, which helps to attenuate mourning their loss. In turn, the meaningfulness of religion is revealed by the many very old, devout, homebound persons who feel abandoned by church or synagogue because they do not participate in formal religious activities nor have clergy or lay visitors. Ending the chapter is a focus on enhancing preservation of self through religion, primarily through increasing collaboration between secular and sectarian sectors on behalf of elderly persons.

Chapter 7, on accepting death, begins with a comment on how death becomes more acceptable at the end of the life course. Then discussed is "terminal drop," the cognitive changes associated with the dying process when old. Whereas preoccupations and fears of death are not associated with terminal drop for those in stable circumstances, for those with "unfinished business" from being in unstable situations, the scenario is different. Thus, three groups with "unfinished business" are discussed: Those in unstable situations such as in the process of becoming institutionalized; those who have responsibilities such as the parents of mentally retarded adult offspring who live with them; and those concerned with not completing self-assigned life goals, as is typical of productive visual artists and other creative individuals. Some implications for practice are discussed and, lastly, the future of accepting death at the end of life.

In Chapter 8, an attempt is made to illustrate beneficial interactions among practice wisdom, research findings and theoretical formulations. Actually, it is a plea to use these perspectives to understand, and to better, the human experience of aging.

It will be readily apparent that practice wisdom has enabled me to generate hypotheses for empirical studies and, in turn, findings from studies have assisted me in the generation of hypotheses for practice. My career in gerontology began in both worlds and has continued in both. Bernice Neugarten, as my research mentor, taught me to simplify without being simplistic, while Jerome Grunes, as my practice mentor, taught me to interpret complexity without becoming convoluted. Together, and synergistically, they taught me how to combine orderly ways of understanding with an openness to new explanations; this combination or orderliness and openness I have tried to apply to all levels of inquiry ranging from elderly individuals in diverse life circumstances to their participation in therapeutic interventions. Additionally, the teachings of my mentors were complementary: Neugarten taught me to understand the diversity of individuals as we examined data gathered from many people, whereas Grunes taught me to understand shared human experiences as we focused on the single individual. Their contributions to me, hopefully, have gained expression in my rudimentary attempt to bridge the worlds of practice and research; and, subsequently, my capacity to inform practitioners of all persuasions on how to make use of an understanding of personhood in advanced old age and to inform researchers on possible directions for future studies.

Fortuitously, I have had the additional rare opportunity to collaborate with Morton A. Lieberman in the quest for understanding adaptational processes in aging. Indeed, the sharing of ideas was such a stimulating and all-engrossing experience that it is impossible to accurately recollect which of us first used the expression "the unique psychology." We emerged with this formulation after many years of immersion in our data, and stimulating discussions regarding their meaning.

Now, in this volume I have attempted to extend this work by an exploration of the usefulness of psychological mechanisms and beliefs for enhancing personhood and, also, to incorporate these processes into a psychodynamic perspective. I have not, however, attempted to be comprehensive. Rather, I have focused on the kinds of older people in the kinds of setting to which I have been exposed. Readers who work with different kinds of elderly in different settings, however, should not have difficulty in extrapolating to their practice. As should have been apparent from my review of the content of the chapters in this preface and as I am sure will soon become apparent from reading these chapters, I have covered a wide variety of the common occurring issues and problems found in working with very old individuals.

I am, as noted above, most grateful to Jerry Grunes, Bernice Neugarten and Mort Lieberman for their intellectual contribution to this book. Many others have also provided me with special kinds of emotional support, especially Vickie Bumagin and Bert Cohler. Thanks are additionally due to Ed Sherman, Max Siporin, Greg Smith, and Ron Toseland who read early drafts and provided helpful constructive criticisms. Executive Editor A. Jean Lesher deserves special acknowledgement as well as her reviewers, as do research assistants Sharon Kirby and Robin Ressler. To B. J. Kelly, my secretary, I owe special thanks for persevering through the retyping of countless drafts. But it is Ursula Springer who has my heartfelt appreciation for publication of this manuscript.

Chapter 1

Psychology of Being "Old"

Being "old" is a state of mind that usually flows from a confluence of age-associated losses such as chronic impairments and death of loved ones. The state of mind is also evidenced among those of advanced age who have suffered fewer age-associated losses but, because of waning energies and an awareness that a lifespan is reaching closure, feel that a threshold has been passed from only being "older" and "elderly" to being "old."

People are indeed aware of the transition so that, for example, labeling oneself as "old" is used to convey a sense of being irreversibly near the end of life—that is, not simply being older or elderly but, rather, being very old, being in advanced old age. The distinction becomes clear when students discuss their respondents in class, which follows the completion of their assignment to interview and then write up a case study of a person living in the community who is 80 years of age or over. Some respondents in their eighties, or even in their nineties, say, "Sure, I'm older than I was and now I'm elderly, but I'm sure as heck not old yet." Others say, "As long as I can move around, I don't feel old." Still others simply say, "I now feel old."

The chronological age at which a person feels "old" varies not only among individuals but also for successive cohorts. Past generations of older persons, for example, may have perceived 70 years of age, "three score and ten," as a demarcation or proxy for oldness. Now with many more persons living and being healthy well beyond 70, the timing for becoming "old" is occurring at later ages. Independent of the age of occurrence, those who perceive themselves as "old" seem to share some common characteristics.

Perceiving oneself as "old" is apparently associated with the acceptance of death (Munnichs, 1966). Instead of a concern with the imminence of nonbeing, there is likely to now be a concern with the process of dying, with a wish not to lose control, be full of pain or to experience death alone. The adaptive task is to still be oneself when confronting the imminence of nonbeing; indeed, the task is to be oneself until the last breath of life.

PRESERVATION OF THE SELF

The primary adaptive task of those now old to preserve the self differs from the primary adaptive task of younger ages, such as of the very young, whose task is to gain a self. It also differs from the primary adaptive task in adulthood, which is to use the self for gratification and to cope with the vicissitudes of life. Although preservation of the self is not the primary adaptive task in childhood and adulthood, an attempt is made throughout life to maintain continuity with the past. In childhood, for example, the gaining of an identity necessitates, according to Erikson (1950), a sense of sameness over time. In turn, in adulthood, adequate functioning in everyday life necessitates a sense of being the same person one has always been. Thus preserving the self is not new because maintaining continuity with the past can be considered a motive throughout the life span. What is different, however, is the centrality of the motive in advanced old age because of the age-associated losses that corrode the sense of self.

The losses in advanced aging occur neither suddenly nor unexpectedly, and are perceived as inherent to a long life. This perception reflects a psychological context remarkably different from that of younger persons. Indeed, young researchers and practitioners can not easily comprehend how it is to live with the kinds of physical impairments and interpersonal losses found among the very old; and certainly, most young people cannot comprehend how it is to live without an active sex life. If such adversities were to occur to them, life would be truly unbearable. Only, however, when they begin to understand and to appreciate aging as a psychosocial process, after interviews with people who are very old, does the concept of being "on time" become real to them. Fortunately, we do not become old suddenly but, rather only after a long life that includes the preceding and usually satisfying young-old years. The task of the old to preserve the self may be similar to the task of younger persons who have a foreshortened life span, and who are aware of the foreshortening. Yet the psychological context of these younger persons is radically different, as it must be for 50-year-old cancer victims who know that their lifespan has not yet been lived and that their deaths are prematurely "off time."

UNIQUE PSYCHOLOGY

Given the heterogeneity among very old people, it is obvious that each person confronts the adaptational task of maintaining the self in his or her own distinct way. Albeit idiosyncratic differences, there still may be shared processes. Thus, the attempt has been to demonstrate that in maintaining their sense of self, those in advanced old age manifest some common psychological processes. To the extent that these processes are shared and also qualitatively different from those found among younger persons, they comprise the unique psychology of the very old.

Unfortunately, individuals have not been studied from youth through old age for how psychological processes used to reaffirm the self are associated with aging. Rather, longitudinal studies of the psychology of aging have focused more on stability of personality traits and on deterioration in functioning. Our own longitudinal studies have focused on how the elderly adapt to the stress of relocation (Lieberman & Tobin, 1983; Tobin & Lieberman, 1976), but the inclusion of control samples not undergoing this stress has facilitated speculation on adaptational processes in aging including the unique psychology of the very old.

In four separate studies, a total of 639 individuals (average age 79 years) were followed from prerelocation to one year postrelocation. Additionally, 198 elderly persons in matched control groups, who were not relocated, were followed during a similar period. Younger control groups were also followed to investigate the specific psychological differences between the young and the old in their use of the present and the past to define current self-concept as well as their use of dramatization to reconstruct reminiscence (Lieberman & Tobin, 1983).

Stability of the Self

The remarkable stability of the self was one of the major findings of these longitudinal studies. In this context, the self refers to the "self-picture" (Rosenberg, 1979), which James (1892) referred to as the "Me." James made a distinction between the self as subject (the "I") and the self as object (the "Me") which was later built upon by Mead (1934).

To assess the content of the self-picture, from before until after relocation, as well as among elderly not being relocated and among younger people, respondents were asked to select from among 48 self-descriptive statements, those that "are like you now." Statements were constructed to tap a wide array of attributes with some positive such as "People think well of me" and "I am a trusting person," but others not, such as "I am somewhat of a dominating or bossy person," and "I can be a cold and unfeeling person." All 48 self-descriptive items were readily intelligible statements. Each item, as well as the set, were generated by using Leary's (1957) interpersonal theory, which provides useful categories for developing self-assessments based on consciously perceived attributes.

The content of self-picture did not change for persons undergoing the stress of relocation nor for those in the control groups not undergoing relocation. That is, respondents in our studies selected the same self-descriptive statements over-time independent of whether undergoing relocation or remaining in their familiar environment.

Interchangeability of the Past and Present

In contrast to the stability of the self-picture, however, validation for the content of the self was found to fluctuate suggesting an interchangeability of evidence from the past and the present. This melding of past and present evidence to support the self concept was remarkably different from evidence used by the younger persons that we studied who relied totally on incidents from their current interpersonal interaction to confirm the self. For example, one elderly woman respondent selected as self-descriptive the statement: "I enjoy being in charge of things." When asked to give examples in the present to validate the statement she vacillated between examples in the present ("Yes! I tell my children when they can come visit me. I told Rose (her daughter) not to come today because you [the interviewer] was coming and I want time to get dressed up.") and in the past ("We had a small jewelry store and I ran it. When my husband was alive we ran it together. When he got sick, I ran it by myself.") In contrast, a high school student always gave a response in the present, such as "I enjoy plenty managing the debating team" and "Right now I'm organizing my club's picnic."

Thus, whereas younger persons readily respond to requests to give current examples to support self-descriptive statements, the elderly vacillate between present examples, past examples, and general statements of conviction. Even when asked in short intervals, such as a week, to give here-and-now examples for a statement chosen, the elderly shift among present examples, examples from the past and comments reflecting conviction. It seems that for elderly persons, evidence from the past and convictions are equivalent to examples from the present in supporting the current self. Moreover, when both the present and the past fail as sources of identity, older persons are willing to forego reality and use evidence based on wishes and distortions to maintain self-consistency.

Distortion Too

An example of distortion is illustrated by the woman in a nursing home who also chose the statement "I enjoy being in charge of things," but the example she gave was "Sure. Here I decide who is boss." Although both the statement and the example contain the dimension of control, her example is not congruent with the statement's meaning of her being in control. Apparently, she is unable to use the institutional environment to provide an example congruent with the statement. Yet, knowing herself to be an "in-charge" person, she selected this item as characteristic of herself.

Persistence of the Self

The blurring of the past and the present in supporting the self is most dramatic when elderly respondents use snapshots taken 50 years ago to explain who they currently are. When this happens to younger interviewers, they initially may think that the elderly respondents have misinterpreted the question pertaining to who they are right now. Then, after repeating the question and the respondent answers "That's me in this picture but I might have changed a little bit," the young interviewer begins to realize that the persons in the snapshot taken 50 years ago is meant to convey the "me in the here-and-now." To the interviewer as he or she begins the interview, the crippled widow of 93 is a frail, impaired old lady who has suffered untold losses. Over the two hour or so interview session, however, the old lady becomes a real person who is the sum of the experience of a long life. The interviewer discovers that for the elderly, identities are persistent (and even, if you wish, eternal).

Too often, however, nonfamily caregivers do not appreciate the inner experience of a persistent identity. Bumagin and Hirn in their 1979 book, *Aging is a Family Affair*, provide a poignant example by reproducing the following poem which was found among the effects of a patient who had died in the Oxford University Geriatric Service Facility in England. The author is unknown.

What Do You See?

What do you see, nurses? What do you see—
Are you thinking, when you are looking at me:
A crabbit old woman, not very wise,
Uncertain of habit, with faraway eyes,
Who dribbles her food, and makes no reply,

When you say in a loud voice, "I do wish you'd try."
Who seems not to notice the things that you do,
And forever is losing a stocking or shoe;
Who unresisting or not lets you do as you will,
When bathing and feeding, the long day to fill.
Is that what you are thinking, is that what you see?
THEN OPEN YOUR EYES, NURSES,
YOU ARE NOT LOOKING AT ME,

I'll tell you who I am, as I sit here so still,
As I rise at your bidding, as I eat at your will.
I'm a small child of ten, with a father and mother,
Brothers and sisters, who love one another;
A young girl of sixteen, with wings on her feet,
Dreaming that soon now a lover she'll meet;
A bride soon at twenty, my heart gives a leap,
Remembering the vows that I promised to keep;
At twenty-five now, I have young of my own,
Who need me to build a secure happy home;
A woman of thirty, my young now grow fast,
Bound to each other, with ties that should last;
At forty my young sons now grow and will be all gone,
But my man stays beside me, to see I don't mourn;
At fifty, once more babies play round my knee,
Again we know children, my loved one and me.
Dark days are upon me, my husband is dead.
I look at the future, I shudder with dread.
For my young are all busy, rearing young of their own,
And I think of the years, and the love that I've known.
I'm an old woman now, and nature is cruel.
It's her jest, to make old age look like a fool.
The body it crumbles, grace and vigour depart,
There is now a stone, where I once had a heart.
But inside this old carcass, a young girl still dwells,

And now and again, my battered heart swells;
I remember the joy, I remember the pain,
And I'm loving and living life all over again.
I think of the years, all too few—gone too fast,
And accept the stark fact that nothing can last.
So open your eyes, nurses, open and see
Not a crabbit old women. Look closer—see ME.   (pp. 193–194)

Just as the woman who wrote this poem retained her identity, so too
did the respondents in our relocation studies. Although their identity
was threatened and by the relocation by loss of people and places and
new demands for adaptation, as well as possibly loss of people and

places and new demands for adaptation, as well as possibly by some awareness of their impending death, they retained a sense of self. Whereas it was expected that the move would limited aged individuals' abilities to maintain a coherent and consistent self-image, they instead showed a remarkable self-image stability, a stability that is comparable to that which is maintained by elderly persons who are not undergoing such upheavals.

Mythicizing the Past

When the reminiscences of older people were compared to those of persons in their middle years, there was a greater degree of dramatization or mythicizing of the past (Revere & Tobin, 1980–81). In this specific investigation, life history data were gathered in face-to-face interviews of approximately three hours' duration. Then older respondents (35 who were 65 to 103 years old) were contrasted with a matched sample of middle-aged persons (25 who were 44 to 55) on 23 scales developed to tap four dimensions: involvement with the past, dramatization of the past, reconciliation with one's past, and consistency in telling one's life story. This analysis revealed only a difference in dramatization. For the older respondents, the family of one's early life becomes "bigger than life"; becomes, that is, portrayed as both more beautiful and as more cruel. Apparently, in the mythicizing of the past, memories are recast to make the uniqueness of the self vivid and, in turn, the myth becomes the reality, and one's life becomes justified.

The vividness of persons in the reconstructions of the past is often in stark contrast to the blandness in the portrayal of self. Indeed, there is usually a rather mundane quality to self reports: "I have always been a family person." "I have made a good living." It is in the reconstruction of now deceased family members, parents, siblings, and spouses that the feelings of specialness emerge: "We were the happiest of families. We all loved each other. My brothers and sisters loved me and I loved them." "My father was a big man, physically. Always wanted us to make a good living, to be a good provider. He didn't do that well, but he was a good provider. Always something on the table. I'm like that."

Lowered Introspection

Another kind of finding that reflects the unique psychology of the very old is a lessening of introspection on feelings. In this study, introspection was assessed by using seven-point scales to rate responses to eight questions on personal feelings. Respondents, for example, were asked, "could you tell me about the times when you feel very lonely?" or "happy," "sad," "proud," and so forth. As association was found between age and unwillingness to introspect on feelings ($r = 0.43$) among 79 elderly persons 68 to 93 years of age. Apparently, as decreasing biological, and thus psychological, energies become deployed for self-maintenance and a sense of sameness is achieved, there is less introspection on, or certainly a preoccupation with, internal feeling states.

Lowered introspection can reflect a resolution of previous lifelong inner conflicts through the acceptance of previously unacceptable, repressed feelings. To illustrate the acceptance of previously unacceptable feelings, psychiatrist Grunes (1968, personal communication) tells about his interview with Mr. Burns, a man is his seventies who never married and had been a rather low-paid salesperson in a department store. When asked to talk about his life, Mr. Burns would say: "I spent my whole life being mad at my brother who was always very successful in everything he did." Then, when asked when this realization occurred to him, responded: "About two years ago. Before that I was always thinking about why I failed and mad at my brother for all his successes. It don't matter so much now."

Allowing Unacceptable Motives Into Consciousness

Other clinicians too have observed that those now old can allow into consciousness some feelings and motives they previously disavowed. Zinberg and Kaufman (1963) note:

> The older patient is far less likely to "kid himself." His awareness of being stirred up by disagreements may be accompanied by a cynical disregard for his own feelings, because he understands himself in a sense too well, but he is more likely to know where the feelings come from and why he is upset. . . . Many feelings which are strongly resisted by younger people are accepted in the aged. The fact that people have destructive and envious urges are often admitted to consciousness without the anxiety and accompanying disorganization that may have occurred if the same feelings had reached awareness earlier in life. . . . They fear the judgment of others less because they see the future as unimportant. (pp. 29–30)

The future judgment of others is a secondary cause for the acceptance of previously repressed material. Rather, as also noted above by Zinberg and Kaufman, the primary cause is a self-understanding. But why with age per se should there be an increase in self-understanding? Is it because self-understanding serves the purpose of preservation of the core self? It is a self-wisdom that is achieved, and not a wisdom regarding regularities in the external world. In the seeking and gaining of a wisdom about the self, a making sense of oneself, there is a selective screening out of reality when warranted and, also, an acceptance of previously unwelcomed motives if they are useful for self-definition. Put another way, the task of the very old to maintain a consistency of self when confronted with losses, which occurs within the awareness of having lived a life and with the acceptance of death, is achieved by a purposeful simplification of identity which reaffirms the self. Accompanying an affirmation of self for many, if not most, Americans, is, as noted earlier, a belief that to live a long life is a "divine reward." Also death itself becomes acceptable and the concern becomes with the process of dying.

LIFESPAN PERSPECTIVE

Throughout the life course there are common age-associated adaptational tasks that are accompanied by shared psychological processes for coping with these tasks. In early childhood, for example, the obvious task of becoming a separate person necessitates that children internalize parental persons. Erikson (1950), to distinguish universal major life tasks from minor, idiosyncratic tasks, preferred the expression "life crises" and labeled each of his eight sequential life crises according to the polar resolutions associated with each task or crisis. The task of the young adult, of "making it" with another person, became "intimacy versus isolation"; of the middle years, of developing a sense of a meaningfully productive person, became "generativity versus stagnation"; and of the last years of life, of accepting one's death, became "integrity versus despair." These Eriksonian life tasks of the adult and later years are not tied as closely to chronological age as are the first five stages he identified for childhood. Rather, adult tasks emerge as crises through accrued experiences and perceptions of one's place in the life cycle. To illustrate, "generativity versus stagnation" is assumed to be a crisis for everyone during their middle years but the precise age of its occurrence will vary. Some in their forties ask themselves if their life has been productive, if they feel generative regarding people and things in which investments have been made. Yet others may not do so until their sixties. Similarly, the last stage of life will depend on those external and internal events that evoke a sense of the end of the life span. Thus, the crisis of "integrity versus despair" will begin at different ages for individuals. Age-associated losses that can not be denied confirm the presence of the final crisis of the life cycle and, as well, its unique psychology.

Cognitive Development

Erikson's descriptions of later life stages are not the only way to concep-tualize how adaptational tasks change after the early formative years. Labouvie-Vief (1985), for example, has discussed how with the attain-ment of adult roles, the orientation toward knowledge shifts from devel-oping cognitive structures and abstract reasoning to using structures and reasoning for specific goals. There is a significant shift in motivation regarding knowledge towards its usefulness in meeting needs. Elderly people are thus likely, in part, to do poorer on tests of intellectual abili-ties and capacities than younger people because of the lack of meaning-fulness of the tests rather than deterioration of their cognitive abilities. A test designed to assess the acquisition of general new knowledge, for example, may be totally irrelevant to elderly people. Other kinds of psy-chological tests may also be irrelevant, such as the TAT (Thematic Ap-perceptive Test) designed to elicit responses to latent stimuli in pictures. Sometimes to older people, the latent become the obvious. I learned this lesson quickly during my clinical training:

I presented a TAT card to a woman in her eighties and asked her, as this test re-quires, to tell a story to the card that depicts a young lad looking at his violin. Whereas the typical respondent begins the story by saying the violin belongs to the boy, this elderly woman in a Jewish Home for the Aged asked: "Is this boy Jewish?" In turn, I asked, "Does it make a difference?" She replied emphati-cally, "Sure!" She then concluded that he was Jewish and proceeded to tell a story about how he became another Heifitz. Had she concluded he was not Jew-ish, she certainly would have told a very different story.

Through Middle Age

Regarding Erikson's next to last, seventh, stage of generativity versus stagnation, there is neither support nor evidence for a crisis or a new major adaptational task between the middle and the final years. What, then, is the nature of change in the middle years which sets the stage for the final shift and, thus, the context for the unique psychology of the very old?

Neugarten and Datan (1973, 1974) reported a shift in the middle years toward what they called "interiority." Between 40 and 60 years of age, people are likely to change in four ways: taking stock of what they have accomplished and what they wish to accomplish in the years to come; a "time reversal" in which time is counted less in terms of years lived and more in terms of years left to live; an identification more with one's parental generation than with one's children's generation; and an awareness of changes in body image. The increasing interiority obviously does not reflect a major personality change, nor does it reflect a mid-life crisis.

Apparently, concurrent with the mid-life shift toward interiority is a movement toward androgyny, toward opposite gender characteristics. Gutmann (1987) has posited that after the parental imperative, women and men begin to accept the opposite gender parts of themselves that have been repressed in the service of child rearing. Women become more aggressive and men more passive. There is evidence for this position. Vaillant (1977), for example, found that men followed from their undergraduate years at Harvard through their early forties became warmer and more open, and Cooper and Gutmann (1987) found that postparental women became more aggressive.

ERIKSON'S LAST STAGE REFORMULATED

Erikson himself reformulated his final psychosocial crisis. In his original theorizing on the last stage of life in *Childhood and Society*, (1950), he postulated that integrity is achieved and despair avoided by accepting life as it has been lived and by investing in the continuity of generations; that is, in investments outside oneself through "secondary narcissism." In 1982, in his advanced old age, Erikson reformulated the last stage of life in his book, *The Life Cycle Completed*, and wrote that integrity,

> in its simplest meaning is, of course, a sense of *coherence* and *wholeness* that is, no doubt, at supreme risk under such terminal conditions as a *loss of linkages* in all three organizing processes: in the soma . . . ; in the psyche, the gradual loss of mnemonic coherence in experience, past and present; and in the Ethos, the threat of a sudden and nearly total loss of responsible function in generative interplay. What is demanded here could simply be called "integrality," a tendency to keep things together. (pp. 64–65)

According to Erikson, a "pseudointegration," rather than an ideal integration, occurs when "retrospective mythologizing" does not contain "a timeless love for those few 'others' who have become the main counterplayers in life's most significant contexts" (p. 65). The secondary narcissism of identification with future generations is no longer in Erikson's formulation, but rather the focus is on reminiscing, reviewing one's life, to achieve coherence and wholeness. Whereas ideal integrity for Erikson necessitates a reminiscence process that includes "timeless love" for significant others, for us this is not at all essential. What is essential is a sense of coherence and wholeness that can be achieved through reminiscence that makes one vivid to oneself in which a sense of the permanent and immutable self is achieved. Coherence and wholeness can be achieved by those who have not known much "timeless love" and whose reminiscence is, unfortunately, filled with vivid and, most likely, accurate memories of losses and deprivation. Yet the person becomes vivid to herself or himself even though Erikson's ideal integrity may never be achieved.

An Illustration

Indeed, Mrs. Edwards, a woman of 86 who described her early, as well as most of her later, life, as only continuous deprivation was able to be proud and filled with self-admiration for having risen above a chaotic and miserable childhood.

Mrs. Edwards' early childhood reads like the most tragic of stories. Her father deserted the family when she was an infant; her mother then became deeply depressed, a sibling died from neglect, she went to live with the classical "wicked stepmother" (in this instance an aunt) who treated her like a servant, her first husband died soon after the birth of her only child, who later became a great disappointment to her, and she married her second husband for convenience. Of him she simply said: "We built a successful business together." Mrs. Edwards' attachments to others were always narcissistic and her relationships can best be characterized as demanding, hostile and suspicious. Her awareness of these traits of herself are revealed not only in her reminiscence and by the self sort items she selected and examples given, but also by her spontaneous comments. For example, when describing the kind of business woman she was (and still sees herself to be) she smiled and said, "I'm not the kind of person anyone should try to cheat. I'm not very nice." Later she commented, "You have to make sure people don't take advantage of you."

To what extent Mrs. Edwards' current self-view contains content that was previously put out of consciousness because it was unacceptable is unclear. Yet, it does appear to the listener that Mrs. Edwards is more accepting of her nastiness now than she had been in her middle years. The awareness of these traits, which possibly were unacceptable earlier in life, are revealed in the self sort statements she selected and the examples given. Moreover, although uneducated, she has gained a self-wisdom in which she relates these traits to her earliest socialization, the content of which is vividly described replete with gory details. Now, at 86, she knows who she is and from where she came. And with an indomitable spirit she knows she will prevail.

RECONSTRUCTIONS OF THE PAST

Note that the past need not be accurate but, rather, it must be made real and vivid. Cohler (1982), after reviewing the literature on reminiscing, provided a synthesis in which he argued that memories are not only continually being reorganized but that a life narrative is created that is not to be judged for its accuracy but rather for its consistency, its coherence, its comprehensiveness and its intelligibility to the listener or reader. For the very old, the life narrative is most importantly the creation of a self story that maximizes their adaptational task as the past is made vivid and as the past and present become blurred so that the continuity of self becomes reaffirmed.

The use of reconstruction of the past for current adaptation is not a new formulation but, rather, it is now being rediscovered as a way of understanding the psychology of aging. Thus, in a recent discussion of adult development and aging for the *Annual Review of Psychology*, the authors (Datan, Rodeheaver, & Hughes, 1988) focused upon and detailed the many current approaches to reminiscence, not only ours but those of others. Some (e.g., Fisseni, 1985) have argued that reconstructions of the past are used by the elderly as evidence for "perceived unchangeability" in coping with constructions in life space from low income, poor health, widowhood and so forth. The now popular "script" theory developed by Tomkins (1986) focuses on how scenes (perceptions of one's life space) become scripts that enable individuals to anticipate, respond to, control, or create events in a meaningful fashion. Developing scripts involves "recruitment of memories, thoughts, actions, and feelings" (Carlson, 1981) in the dynamic interaction between early events and current perceptions where early events affect current perceptions and, in turn, current perceptions affect the reconstruction of early events. Yet, as revealed by in our data (Revere & Tobin, 1980/81), very old people are involved differently with their past.

One fascinating example of this involvement occurred in a discussion with a world renown sociologist in his late eighties.

Professor Lerner asked me if it is still believed that whereas memory fails in advanced aging, remote memory remains constant. He then related how he has noticed how elderly relatives have modified their memories to incorporate current concerns. That is, when happy, the reconstructed event was elaborated upon with pleasantness but when sad, the same event took on a depressive tone. But later in the conversation, he shared his real concern. He has become increasingly aware that early memories have been pushing into consciousness and also that there is a kind of mutability to them so that sometimes he felt that his recall of early events was becoming distorted. I assured him that memories are always changing and, also, that there is evidence that they become more vivid. With great relief, he soon discussed his earliest memory that included his mother and then elaborated upon a quite vivid recollection of her. Apparently, the mutability and vividness of resurgent early memories had greatly disturbed this introspective and perceptive man who could cope with losses in immediate memory but not with the changes in recollections of early memories which he interpreted as some kind of destructuralization.

Unlike many others his age, Professor Lerner is highly introspective, but, in common with most other persons of advanced age, he illustrates the active involvement in memories that are dramatic and vivid but also continually changing as present adaptive concerns become incorporated into recollections.

STABILITY OF THE SELF

Surely, stability of the self is not a new idea. Cicero, in 44 B.C., wrote his essay "De Senectute" ("On Old age") when he was 62, a rather advanced age 2000 years ago. In this dialogue, two younger men pose their questions to Marcus Procius Cato, the wise elder of 84:

> Scipio, aged thirty-five, opens the conversation by saying to Cato: "I have never noticed that you find it wearisome to be old. That is very different from most other old men, who claim to find their age a heavier burden than Mount Etna itself." Cato responds, "A person who lacks the means, within himself, to live a good and happy life will find any period of his existence wearisome. But rely for life's blessings on your own resources, and you will not take a gloomy view of any of the inevitable consequences of nature's laws. Everyone hopes to attain an advanced age; yet when it comes they all complain! . . . Old Age, they protest, crept up on them

more rapidly than they had expected . . . who was to blame for their mistaken forecast? For age does not steal upon adults any faster than adulthood steals upon children . . . I follow and obey nature as a divine being. Now since she has planned all the earlier divisions of our lives excellently, she is not likely to make a bad playwright's mistake of skimping the last act. And a last act was inevitable. There had to be a time of withering, of readiness to fall, like the ripeness which comes to the fruits of the trees and of the earth. But a wise man will face this prospect with resignation, for resistance against nature is as pointless as the battles of the giants against the gods." (Cicero, 44 B.C., pp. 214–215)

The difference between those who are wise and those who are unwise is suggested here and elsewhere by Cicero to be a personality disposition; that is, a characteristic inculcated early in life that persists throughout life. The obvious stability of basic personality is, however, not incompatible with the obvious changes in behaviors as we adapt to new roles, drop other roles and modify the content of still other roles as new demands emerge. We behave differently, for example, as a young child of a healthy mother than we do when caring for a frail mother in her eighties. Yet, at our core, there is persistence of the self, of our identities.

There have been, however, those who have questioned the extent of stability in old age. Cumming and Henry (1961), for example, developed the disengagement hypothesis. It is natural, they argued, to disengage from one's social world in preparation for death. This view was in opposition to Havinghurst and Albrecht's (1953) activity theory in which it was assumed that the maintenance of high activity levels are necessary to counteract the losses associated with aging. Data, however, from the first large-scale cross-sectional study of persons 45 years and older, the Kansas City Studies of Adult Lives, suggested that neither theory was adequate to explain lives of the aging, and specifically successful aging. Rather, we (Havinghurst, Neugarten, & Tobin, 1968) introduced personality dimensions as most crucial in explaining successful aging. As Neugarten (1977) later put it:

From a social psychological perspective aging is better viewed not as a process of engagement or disengagement, but as a process of adaptation in which personality is the key element. The aging individual not only plays an active role in adapting to the biological and social changes that occur with the passage of time, but in creating patterns of a life that will give him greatest ego involvement and life satisfaction. (p. 643)

Note that whereas Neugarten shares with Cicero the view that individual differences determine adaptations to aging, she additionally emphasizes the proactive nature of adaptation, the creating of life that enhances oneself. In turn, because we are all different, the selves we seek to enhance vary among us. Indeed, the differences among people, the heterogeneity in our samples, is what was impressive, rather than any similarity because of a common age.

Continuity of the Self

So, too, the sociologist Atchley (1971), in studying adaptation to retirement, discovered remarkable differences in adaptation rather than commonalities, which led him to formulate his "continuity theory." Meanwhile, psychologists Costa and McCrea (1984) discovered remarkable stability of personality traits through adulthood into the young-old years; also a Sense of Coherence Model was developed (Antonovsky, 1979); and then Kaufman (1987) quite successfully illustrated how older persons transform experience into themes that provide a persistence to self-meaning. Most recently, Atchley (1989) has developed a fuller "continuity theory," by elaborating upon how motives to maintain inner continuity shape behavior. Here, in turn, the quest has been to identify those psychological mechanisms used by those now "old" to maintain continuity and to preserve the self.

Preserving a persistent self is obviously related to perceiving life-long stability in the self. Mischel (1969) has written: "The experience of subjective continuity in ourselves—of basic oneness and durability in the self—is perhaps the most compelling and fundamental feature of personality" (p. 1012). The experience of continuity, however, may be illusionary, which Mischel recognized following a review of the literature. He continued: "Indeed we do not need to recognize that discontinuities—real ones and not merely superficial veneer changes—are part of the genuine phenomenon of personality."

Longitudinal studies, in turn, support some kind of continuity. Haan and her group (Haan, 1976; Haan & Day, 1974), for example, showed that traits classified as reflecting the self-concept, in contrast to information processing skills, interpersonal relations and responses to socialization, were the most stable from adolescence through the middle years. Regardless of the extent of actual stability that exists throughout the life span, there is agreement that people strive to maintain the content of the self, to maintain identity. Self theorists have made the preservation of the self primary in human motivation. To them the self is not simple self-esteem but one's "self picture." It is the self-picture that is to be maintained and the process of maintenance may be different among the very old than for younger people. But why should processes of maintenance of the content of the self be different for the very old?

Social Interaction in Maintenance of the Self

Investigators of how the self is maintained earlier in life have focused on how current interaction is used to maintain and support the self. One expert (Swann, 1983), for example, in synthesizing the experimental findings related to the maintenance of the self among younger persons elaborated on two processes. First, an "opportunity structure . . . is developed in which signs and symbols are displayed to evoke affirmation of the self, interaction is selected with the kinds of people and in the kinds of situations that will provide confirmation, and interpersonal prompts are adapted to elicit confirmatory reactions." Secondly, current social interaction is perceived as self-confirmatory by selective attention, by recalling the kinds of information that provides confirmation, and by interpreting interaction as congruent with the content of the self. Even, however, when these self-confirmatory processes are available to the very old in their current environment, they may rely more on the past for confirmatory evidence. For the very old, current self image which is anchored in an overall assessment of one's life, as well as in a lengthy past in which significant life roles were enacted, can provide the assurance of immediate meaning and continuity to current existence.

Relying on the Past

Throughout life, the past is always used for self validation. In old age, however, the past is not only used more and made more vivid, but, also, there is an apparent blurring of the present and the past in self-validation. In discussing why the very old rely more on the past rather than social comparisons in the present, two prominent social psychologists (Suls & Mullen, 1982) offered three explanations: a lack of interpersonal relatedness, a lack of cognitive strength for social comparisons, and a reduction in the importance of self-evaluations. Although their explanation of a reduction in the importance of self-evaluations is not supported by the literature, the other two explanations apparently are supported. First, for many elderly, there is a lack of opportunities to interact with meaningful others in roles that may have been lost through death of others or through age-associated loss, such as the end of child-rearing or retirement. And, secondly, for many older persons who do not manifest a serious lack of cognitive strength, as reflected in disorientation and confusion, their interpretations of physical and cognitive decrements may be a limiting factor. That is, when it is believed by an elderly person that he or she can no longer manipulate or structure present interactions because of decrements, even when the decrements are not so debilitating that they negate interpersonal structuring, the individual may increasingly rely on the past for self-affirmation.

Using the Past

Those in advanced old age, in using the past to maintain the self, are not aware of the many adverse changes that have impinged upon their identity. The 87-year-old woman who acknowledges to herself that she is withered and even unattractive may at the same time feel herself to be the attractive petite beauty who was the apple of her father's eye. In evoking this memory she retains the convictions of her identity. One example is the woman of 84 who reported that her earliest memory was of how her father rode his big white horse into the village when she was about 3 or 4, swept her up, placed her upon his shoulder, and rode around the village square with her perched high on his shoulder so that everyone could see his beautiful daughter. In perceiving herself as still the same person she has been from her earliest years of life, it becomes possible for her to retain her core identity. With the nearness of death being recognized, her whole life can become integrated with a personal wisdom regarding the unity of her life.

Although there is a recognition of the importance of reminiscence in reinforcing the self, Erikson cautioned that a "retrograde mythicizing" should not be interpreted as integrity. Empirical evidence, however, does not support this perspective but, in agreement with another perspective offered by Erikson, there may be a "generalization of sensual modes" which can foster "an enriched bodily and mental experience even as heart functions weakens and genital energy diminishes" (p. 65). This too, however, is not separate from early life experience. In the very act of giving oneself sustenance, in the very act of eating, the very old not only are nourishing themselves and enjoying food, but are also using the occasion to reminisce about food and sustenance and its meaning throughout life. To use a cliche, eating itself becomes "food for thought." Therefore, our memories are important to us at any age, but their usefulness for the very old makes the reminiscence processes qualitatively different.

Although perceptions of stability may be useful to people of all ages and circumstances, this phenomenon, apparently, has rarely been systematically investigated. One exception is Handel's (1984) investigation of how various groups of adults, but none beyond middle-aged, confirm their stability by comparing the present to the past. He found that ubiquitous appraisals of favorable futures are constructed to maintain stability in the future. This may be so for the middle aged, but perceiving a favorable future is a less likely possibility for the very old. Middle-aged respondents with a foreshortened lifespan, however, such as those with a recurrence of cancer, may be more like the very old, where there is a poignancy about the present and an unfavorable future, with the past used as a source of comfort.

ADAPTATION TO STRESS

The thrust of this chapter to this point has been on the normative psychology of the oldest old and, more specifically, on how the self is preserved among those who now consider themselves to be "old." The psychological mechanisms useful for preservation of the self, such as using the past interchangeable with the present and making the past vivid, do not alone reduce vulnerability to severe stressors such as relocation.

Aggressiveness

Most critical to resisting the adverse effects of crisis is aggressiveness. That is, assertiveness, even combativeness, in interactions with the external world facilitates adaptation to stress. Thus those who apparently can evade the developmental push toward increased passivity in advanced old age are better equipped to cope with stress.

A writer for *Science 85* (Wacker, 1985) presented our finding in this way:

> Everybody in the old-age home loved Mary Frances. In her late seventies, she was cheerful, undemanding, cooperative. She went out of her way to help other residents in the little Midwestern home, sewing for a woman whose fingers were stiff with arthritis, writing letters for another whose eyesight was failing. She kept up with a large circle of friends outside the institution and was a regular at the kaffeeklatch. Although a hip operation

had left her with a slight limp, and arthritis had settled in her knees, she rarely complained. When the operators of the home announced that they would have to close and the 45 residents would be relocated to a larger, more impersonal institution, she took the news better than most patients. "I'm not happy about it," she told an interviewer, "but I'm sure it will work out for the best. There will be things in the new place we'll like better than here."

Shortly after the move Mary Frances was bedridden and listless; in six months she was dead.

After relocation, she lapsed into what psychologists call the first-month syndrome, a common institutional malady caused by a change of environment. She sank into deep depression; she began to complain about the pain in her arthritic knees. For patients who can adjust to new surroundings, the depression lifts, and the frequent complaints of minor pains gradually cease. For Mary Frances, they did not. Her depression deepened into apathy. Some days she wouldn't leave her bed. She seemed never to recover her old spirit and finally, one gray day, as unpromising as the previous one, she died.

Harry was something else again. The day he entered his old-age home at eighty-one he complained to a social worker about the racial makeup of the staff. A few weeks later, he drove a volunteer aide out of his room in tears, accusing her of having stolen his false teeth. "You probably hocked 'em!" he shouted at her.

He boasted to everyone around him that he had beaten up his top sergeant in the army 60 years earlier, "and I could do it again if I wanted to, by God!" He refused to bathe regularly and carried so strong a scent of urine that other patients shrank from him in the halls. He proudly attributed this avoidance to their fear of his physical strength.

A bachelor, he was persuaded to enter the home by his only relative, a young woman. She convinced him that he needed close medical attention because of a serious heart condition and emphysema. She helped him move in and at first visited him frequently. But then they had a disagreement over politics, and he ordered her to leave and never come back. She continued to call, but he refused to speak to her.

Eight years after being taken to the home, despite his heart condition and worsening emphysema, Harry roared on, ignoring or feuding with his fellow patients and abusing staff members, who whispered to each other that he was "just too mean to die."

Why did Harry, ill, suspicious, and hostile, apparently thrive in an environment similar to that which felled Mary Frances, originally far healthier and more hopeful? Two University of Chicago psychologists, Morton Lieberman and Sheldon Tobin, became interested in questions like this 21 years ago, when a study they were doing on stress and the elderly turned up mortality results that surprised them. With disturbing consistency, the "wrong" old people were dying. The surly and paranoid survived, while the cheerful, cooperative, seemingly mentally healthy succumbed. (p. 64)

Successful adaptation to stress by the elderly, thus, was associated with aggressiveness, not giving into lethal passivity. But why did the nasty folks do better? Nastiness per se is not the critical predictor of intact survivorship to stress but, rather, it is not letting oneself become passive. Passivity leads to adverse outcomes not only among the very old who are undergoing stress but also among younger persons. Particularly for older people, nonpassivity or mobilization is necessary under stress because of physical vulnerability. Slight imbalances can overtax biological systems that have little residual homeostatic capacity leading to a rapidly accelerating downward course. Elderly persons who are non-passive and mobilized tend not to blame oneself for unavoidable losses which at any age leads to depression. It is indeed appropriate and proper to rage at the fates; and it is better even to project the blame onto others than to blame oneself. Blaming others, specifically loved ones, serves an additional psychological purpose because it is also an expression of the plea for help when actually the kind of help wanted cannot be forthcoming, that is, the regaining of lost health and, for some, the restoring to life of loved ones lost to death.

Aggressiveness is thus often a very human way of coping with adversities over which we have no control. At one level, the aggressiveness reflects the necessary mobilization to cope with stress; at another level, aggressiveness reflects the appropriate anguish of a desperate situation; and at still another level, aggressiveness reflects our most human of wishes for others, and particularly loved ones, to rescue us from intolerable circumstances. Unfortunately, life stresses can evoke basic fears of helplessness from a malevolent environment where there is little probability of being rescued. Then, aggressiveness, including ventilation of rage, which may be manifested as functional paranoia (Perlin & Butler, 1963), can reduce hopelessness and eventuate a better adaptation to stress.

Magical Coping

Also helpful in reducing the vulnerability to the stress of relocation was the use of magical coping. As reported in the 1976 Tobin-Lieberman book *Last Home for the Aged*, when residents-to-be were assessed before relocation, it was found that those who transformed the situation so as to make the move totally voluntary and also to perceive their relocation environment as ideal were those most likely to survive intact through one year following admission. A similar kind of magical mastery, making life manageable through magical thinking, was observed but Gutmann (1964, 1987) in his TAT studies of normative aging. Whereas young adults handled the latent conflicts expressed in TAT cards through active mastery and adults in their middle years through passive mastery, the oldest cohorts used magical mastery to cope with inner tensions and perceived conflicts in the external world. In our studies, magical coping, as well as aggressiveness, was found to enhance adaptation in all four relocation situations as reported in the Lieberman-Tobin 1983 book *The Experience of Old Age*.

Perceiving the relocation environment as being congruent with the ideal environment and making relocation a voluntary decision have, in common with the reconstruction of reminiscence, a quality of "myth-making." The elderly respondents initially did not assess the situation as either containing a relocation environment at all congruent with their ideal environment nor as one in which they had much control. To transform perceptions so that the relocation becomes welcomed and voluntary suggests not only mythicizing, a magical controlling of reality, but also a disregard for reality. This disregard was also reflected in mechanisms for validating the current self-concept; figures from the past were mythicized.

Magical coping, is apparently also functional for younger persons. Taylor (1989) has recently provided evidence for the importance of what she has labeled "cognitive illusion." In her studies of breast cancer patients, she found that it was common to maintain an illusion of mastery of the disease, and that illusions of conquering the disease through personal behaviors were associated with better adaptation and even longer survival. She argues that positive mental health is characterized not by accurate appraisals of reality but rather by self-enhancing illusions. It is certainly not new to the literature that people of all ages exaggerate their importance and also feel they have more control of their lives than they do. Paradoxically, those who are depressed may be more realistic about their lives and their abilities to control their lives than the more mentally healthy. Indeed, it may be the most mentally healthy individuals who can maintain positive illusions in everyday life and also use magical coping when under stress. Taylor may be correct; it is probably quite difficult for those of us who received their clinical training in the 1960s to accept that distorting of reality is associated with positive mental health. Did not Jahoda in her 1963 book *Current Concepts of Positive Mental Health* make the accurate perception of reality a cardinal indicator of positive mental health?

Intrinsic to self-enhancing illusions, to magical coping, is a sense of control of forces external to oneself. Personal control has been a favorite topic of psychologists in the 1980s. Most pertinent is the research by Rodin and Langer (best summarized in Langer's 1989 book *Mindfulness*). Giving institutionalized elderly people even small degrees of control, such as a choice of entrees when before there was no choice, was associated with enhanced well-being and also with a lengthening of survival. Clearly, for those who have lost their sense of control, providing rather simple, prosaic choices can lead to their regaining positive illusions.

A sense of control is common to the very old and inseparable from the preservation of self, as was quickly discovered by our interviewers:

Mrs. Wexler, an obese 81-year-old widow in the control group (those who had not applied for admission to nursing homes) was placing herself in danger by persisting in living in a third floor apartment. Her physician insisted that she move because walking up the stairs even once a day was taxing her already weakened heart. She left her apartment a few times a day to shop and to participate in activities in the community with her friends. When asked why she would not move, she said to the interviewer, who was 43, "Honey, when you slept in the same bed with your husband for half a century, you don't change it easily." She then communicated that it was better to die in her own bed in familiar surroundings than relocate and be miserable, and added, "If I want to risk it, it's my business. Ain't a little exercise always good for you? And I know better than my doctor what's good for me and what my heart can take. It's only a few steps and he makes it a big thing, like it's the Taj Mahal or something."

Although the interviewer feared for Mrs. Wexler's health, she was sufficiently perceptive not to interfere in any way with Mrs. Wexler's rationalization for the health-producing stair climbing that was interpreted by Mrs. Wexler in a later interview as "Only a little exercise. You need it too. I saw how you couldn't catch your breath when you got up here."

Hopefulness

In the relocation studies, hopefulness also reduced vulnerability to stress. Both aggressiveness and magical mastery reflect hopefulness or, at least, an attempt to reestablish hopefulness. Yet, of interest, too much hopefulness can lead to adverse consequences. Hopefulness in the absence of aggressiveness and magical coping becomes a false hopefulness that can easily be thwarted when conditions do not improve. It may be similar to the unrealistic hopefulness in Elizabethan ballads where love is too easily thwarted when expectations are too highly un-realistic. Still, to have hope, even when it appears unrealistic to all those around you, is helpful in resisting stress.

RELIGIOUS BELIEFS

Because of religious beliefs, persons of advanced old age can feel per-sonally blessed by God for having lived a life. Moreover, more than 7 of 10 Americans (Gallup & Castelli, 1989) believe in an afterlife. For them, the afterlife contains reunions with deceased loved ones. These antici-pated reunions attenuate mourning and also provide an optimistic fu-ture (see Chapter 6).

ACCEPTANCE OF DEATH

Even those who do not believe in an afterlife can, apparently, accept their own death. Although an existential dread of death (Kierkegaard, 1844) may be shared by all human beings, it is likely to be manifest among persons in their middle years rather than when very old. In ad-vanced old age, the preoccupation is usually with the process of dying and not with death itself. The kinds of older people, however, who are likely to fear nonbeing will be included in the discussion of the accept-ance of death in Chapter 7.

WELL-BEING

Does the acceptance of death, as well as religious beliefs and psycholog-ical mechanisms that maintain the self among very old people protect and enhance their feelings of well-being? Whereas many elderly per-sons report some depressive symptoms, such as loneliness and blue moods, there is no more clinical depression among elderly persons than among persons of younger ages (Blazer et al., 1987; Gurland et al., 1980). Put simply, very old people may have some more unhappy feel-ings than younger people, but more of them are not deeply (clinically) depressed (about 2% to 6% depending on measures used and study populations). Yet the absence of depression is not the only way to assess well-being.

Life Satisfaction

Discontent with using measures of well-being that were developed for younger people, we (Neugarten, Havinghurst, & Tobin, 1961) developed a life satisfaction measure more appropriate for elderly persons. This measure of life satisfaction consisted of five scales: zest versus apathy, resolution and fortitude, congruence between desired and achieved goals, self-concept, and mood. No association was found between age and life satisfaction for persons aged fifty and over in the Kansas City Study of Adult Lives. Mood did show some decline with age but was balanced by the other four dimensions, particularly by the congruence between desired and achieved goals. This kind of finding emerged later from a national survey (Campbell, Converse, & Roger, 1976) because those over 65, as compared to younger adults, reported less happiness but more satisfaction with life.

In shifting with age from happiness to satisfaction, it is apparent that disappointments become accepted as part of life. It is not possible to live to a very advanced age without losses. According to George Pollock (1987), normative processes entail mourning losses in which there is a freeing from their consequent preoccupations and depression. When resolved, these mourning experiences become part of a long life filled with vicissitudes. Not uncommon is to be told by an octogenarian, "My life, in balance, has been a good life, a life worth living. Sure, there have been lost opportunities and paths taken that have led to nowhere. But you learn to accept that. You learn that the good outweighs the bad." The "bad" is not disavowed. Nor do the conflicts, as well as the unacceptable motives underlying the conflicts, necessarily dissolve. They often do, but when they do not, like for the most psychologically healthy among us, they neither distort nor disturb us.

"The Rich and Famous Lady"

Despite the evidence for well-being among the elderly, the distortion persists that they are generally unhappy and dissatisfied. Indeed, older people are often characterized as bored and apathetic. It then becomes our job to stimulate them. Yet, if the task of those now old is to be the same people they have always been and if they have always been, for example, nonintellectual, it is not our task to make them intellectual, curious, creative, and so forth. An example:

Mrs. Bates is an 80-year-old widow who lives alone in a big, decaying house in a rural area. Her only child, a son, lives far away and although he phones her about once a month, he has not visited in "three or four years." A senior center provides her with a hot lunch each day and, by careful planning, she stretches this meal throughout the day. She is homebound, preferring not to navigate her front steps because of fears of falling. An episode of syncope following a change in "heart pills" has induced her to avoid moving around. Her main activity is watching TV, especially *The Lives of the Rich and Famous*. Indeed, Mrs. Bates continually introjected anecdotes about the rich and famous into her answers to interviewer's questions. Only after promising that she would have ample time to talk about her favorites after the interview, did she agree to stick with the questions.

Her animated report on her favorites revealed an almost bibliographic accounting of everyone who was ever featured on the TV program. The interviewer, who had never watched the program, sat spellbound and began to realize that Mrs. Bates was not an inert vacuous lady.

It then emerged that the meals-on-wheels people linger to hear her animated, gossipy reports and also that she has a network of friends who chat daily on the phone about the latest people featured on the program.

Mrs. Bates, labeled by us "The Rich and Famous Lady," is obviously neither rich nor famous. She may be considered by some to be living in a dream world with only vicarious thrills. But regardless of her reasons for immersion in the world of the rich and famous, her mind is active and she feels satisfied with her life. When it comes to evaluating the lives of others, we must be cautious in our judgments and recognize the old adage: "different strokes for different folks."

INTEGRATING PERSONHOOD INTO PRACTICE

The contents of this chapter on the psychology of the old can, and should, be integrated into practice. How it can be integrated into practice will, however, vary by characteristic of clients or patients, workers or therapists, and settings. Some of the variations will be discussed in the chapters that follow. But it is only a beginning. The content, including illustrative vignettes, should only be read as an introduction to the meaningfulness of considering how general principles derived from the qualities personhood in advanced old age can be incorporated into practice. Hopefully, therefore, each reader will decide for him or herself how to modify practice. A conscious attempt, therefore, has been made not to be too prescriptive; that is, not to flesh out in detail how readers should modify their practice. One reason for this conscious decision is the diversity among practitioners in their orientations to practice. Although the many aspects of the psychology of those now "old" may be relevant for the diversity of practitioners, how practitioners with different orientations incorporate these aspects can be expected to vary. Yet, as will become apparent, psychodynamically oriented therapists may use the past differently with the very old, to affirm the self rather than to promote insights or to resolve conflicts; cognitive therapists may accept more magical coping; and behavioral therapists may choose not to extinguish seemingly dysfunctional behaviors. It is thus, to a great degree, left to each practitioner to decide how best, or appropriate it is, to incorporate one or another aspect of personhood into his or her practicing, which, hopefully, will become evident as the focus now turns to counseling individuals.

Chapter 2
Applying Therapeutic Approaches

This chapter begins by illustrating the congruence between psychological processes used by those now "old" and therapeutic approaches developed by two skilled, experienced psychoanalysts. Discussed next are the beneficial uses of mobilizing aggression, of making the past vivid, and of magical coping. The chapter continues with sections on the limits of supportive psychotherapy, specifically when there is a need for action and not words; on the usefulness of reconstructive psychotherapy; and on how practitioners modify their practice with elderly individuals, incorporating discussion of transference and countertransference issues. The chapter ends with a rhetorical question: So, why work with old people?

USE OF THE UNIQUE PSYCHOLOGY IN THERAPY

The usefulness in therapy of understanding how personhood is preserved by the unique psychology of the very old is graphically illustrated by the therapeutic approaches of two psychoanalysts, both of whom were consultants in homes for the aged for over three decades: Goldfarb, at the Hebrew Home and Hospital in New York City, and Grunes, at the Drexel Home for the Aged in Chicago. Goldfarb (1959) has focused on enhancing magical coping, on what he has called "inflating" beliefs in mastery. Grunes (1982), in turn, has focused on facilitating organized, vivid reconstructions of the past.

Reestablishing Organized Memories

Grunes (1982) has written:

> Patient and therapist must work to recover past memories and this work
> must be an active therapeutic maneuver involving interventions and re-
> constructions of such memories for the patient. The therapist must permit
> himself the luxury of regression so that in his own psychic apparatus he
> can perceive the patient not only as he exists in the present but visualize
> him as he existed in the past, while conveying to the patient his experi-
> ences with such regressive imago. This is the essence of the therapeutic
> experience. The patient, bewildered and in need of touchstones, can find,
> with the uncovering and the attempt to reestablish memories from his
> own life with a nonjudgmental person, a recathexis of his own past and a
> sufficient organization of the historical sense of self, perhaps less subtly
> organized but organized nonetheless, to function as a unified
> personality. . . . It is the recathectic memories reincorporated with the
> sense of worthwhileness that the patient receives from the therapist.
> (p. 547)

This approach in psychotherapy shares much with Butler's (1963)
therapeutic intervention based on his model of the "life review." Yet it is
also quite different because the focus for Grunes is not on resolving past
conflicts. Rather, Grunes agrees with Cohler (1982) that the experience
of the past when very old is best conceptualized as a series of reconstructions in which the elderly person abstracts from the past those
memories that reaffirm the uniqueness of self. Whereas reconstructions
of the past are always used for current adaptational purposes, for those
now old, the most important use is for preservation of the self.

Inflating Beliefs

Goldfarb (1959), on the other hand, in focusing on enhancing mastery
in the external world, wrote:

> Treatment efforts may therefore be directed toward augmenting the pa-
> tient's ability to master problems . . . or toward inflating his belief that he
> can and does master current problems. (p. 386).

He adds:

> Anxiety can have an organizing effect by increasing alertness and promot-
> ing action. Anxiety may be followed by anger which exerts an organizing

action, and which, in addition, tends to enhance the individual's sense of strength and pride. (p. 386)

And later in the chapter continues:

Because he feels that interest in displayed in him, the person comes to believe that he has won, charmed, tricked, or otherwise gained the social advantage. The receipt of medicine, assistance in environmental manipulation or acceptable advice within acceptable ranges is often taken as a token or symbol of having gained the therapist as ally, friend, or protector, and, simultaneously, as proof of having triumphed over, or having dominated him. This sense of triumph, of having won the therapist's powers and of owning them, may be carried out of each session; a parent figure has been incorporated. (p. 393)

And finally:

To encourage acceptance of limitations and disability is to foster self-recrimination and loss of self-respect; it encourages regarding oneself as crippled and weak. (p. 394)

Facilitating Mythmaking

In Goldfarb's augmenting of his elderly patients' feelings of potency and in Grunes' reviving the reconstruction of organized memories of his elderly patients, both psychotherapists are facilitating mythmaking. As discussed in the previous chapter, mythmaking is inherent to beliefs in one's greater mastery than is realistic and also to reconstructing the past wherein significant others become bigger than life heros and anti-heros. In these mythmaking processes in psychotherapy with the elderly, as in their spontaneous occurrence among the very old, the reality principle recedes in importance: Grunes refers to a "historical sense of self" that is "less subtly organized," and Goldfarb to "inflating" a belief in mastery. Less critical, therefore, than strict adherence to reality is that these mechanisms preserve the self.

Shared also by both therapists is the importance of enhancing self-worth. For Grunes, self-worth is evoked by the therapist while re-cathecting the past, whereas for Goldfarb, self-worth comes from identification with the powers of the therapist and from beliefs in one's personal powers to transcend limitations. Anger for Goldfarb becomes useful in this process, particularly in "organizing action," which is not unlike one kind of rationale for the benefits of aggressiveness to very old people when confronting life crises.

Compatibility of Approaches

The approaches of Goldfarb and Grunes are compatible and, actually, each approach leads to the explicit goal of the other approach. The 87-year-old woman who regains her sense of narcissism by recapturing memories of a father who "loved me best of all" is also reestablishing a belief that those in her current environment recognize her when she wears a pretty dress, and then interpreting, and often misinterpreting, responses to her as admiration, appreciation and love. In turn, when Goldfarb has discussed how his urging the woman in her ninth decade whose hands are crippled with arthritis to return to knitting, it becomes obvious that he had very purposively selected a meaningful activity from her past that provides her a way of organizing and structuring her memories. Whereas Goldfarb used this case to illustrate how the reestablishment of a rather mundane activity can help move a patient from depression and dependency toward exaggerated feelings of mastery and independence, the interaction also includes a recathexis of the past in which the elderly woman became more vivid to herself.

Thus, the approaches of Goldfarb and Grunes are mutually reinforcing. At the simplist level, both use talking cures (variably referred to as psychotherapy, treatment or counseling) to provide crisis management, or supportive therapy, for those elderly persons in advanced age who are experiencing psychological stress. Whereas Goldfarb focused on the inability to reestablish beliefs in control of the external environment, Grunes focused on the inability to maintain an organized reconstruction of the past. Inabilities to retain inflated beliefs in control and to organize vivid reconstructions of the past are symptoms of inner psychological stress, particularly among the very old. In supportive therapy with an empathic clinician, the reestablishment of adapted inflated beliefs in mastery reduces the disorganizing psychological stress, permitting a recathexis of past memories in an organized and vivid manner. In turn, the empathic clinician who facilitates a reorganization of recollections, by reducing inner stress, facilitates coping with the external world.

Above all, shared by both therapists is a therapeutic optimism. Whereas some therapists emphasize, as Yalom (1987), "the loss of possibility" and as Nemiroff and Colarusso (1985) "the race against time," and still others, as Berezin (1987), "ego depletion," for Grunes and for Goldfarb, narcissistically injured, frail, elderly individuals can be helped to transcend these realities. And, in my perspective, we can do so by encouraging the use of the normative psychological mechanisms that are employed by those now old: Mobilizing aggressiveness, making the past vivid, and enhancing magical coping.

MOBILIZING AGGRESSIVENESS

The importance of aggressiveness in treating the very old was demonstrated many years ago by Brody, Kleban, and their colleagues (Brody et al., 1971; Kleban et al., 1971). This group found that aggressiveness was necessary to reduce excess disability among mentally impaired elderly persons institutionalized in a home for the aged, the Philadelphia Geriatric Center. Excess disabilities, which refer to discrepancies in functional incapacity that are greater than that warranted by actual impairments, were identified for thirty two pairs of female residents in the experimental study. Then an individualized treatment plan was designed for one of each pair (the experimental group) aimed at reducing their excess disabilities. Only among those who were nonpassive, who were sufficiently aggressive, were excessive disabilities reduced. Kleban et al. (1971) reported that

> the fact remains that certain personality characteristics described with the "aggression factor" were strongly predictive of the treatment potential of these individuals. . . . Aggressive, stubborn, non-conforming individuals elicit negative reactions from others and therefore tend to be regarded as maladjusted; difficult, and inflexible. They may be viewed as unpleasant, undisciplined children in the conscious and unconscious attitudes of the staff. They may be all these things, but our data suggest very clearly that within this aggressive behavior is a force for self improvement. . . . It may be these "fighters" who become management problems rather than yield to a structured environment. They, rather than the "adjusted" people improved when direction and means of implementation were given to help them to retrieve functions that had been important in previous years. (p. 139)

Thus, unless more passive elderly individuals become aggressive, even the best of therapeutic intentions and interventions may fail. Note that the factor of "aggressiveness" that was associated with therapeutic success was not simply mobilization, or nonpassivity, but rather a kind of determined nastiness that usually alienates others. Indeed, it is the same kind of aggressiveness that was found to insulate the very old from the deleterious effects of stress, as discussed in the previous chapter. Specific illustrations of mobilizing aggressiveness will be included throughout later chapters.

MAKING THE PAST VIVID

Early in my clinical training, I learned the importance of helping patients to make their pasts vivid to themselves. Because, as part of my training in clinical psychology, I was to become familiar with the variety of projective techniques, my psychologist supervisor asked me to administer a battery of psychological tests to a depressed woman in her mid-eighties.

When I showed Mrs. Davis the first Rorschach card, she became rather agitated and said: "What has this got to do with me?" At that moment, I, too, wondered what the purpose of projective tests were. To be sure, one of the didactic experiences I was to gain was an appreciation of the kinds of projective tests most sensible for very old individuals. Yet, regardless of the nature of her intrapsychic conflicts, it was apparent that this woman was suffering from her deep sorrow. So, I put aside the testing material and simply asked her what was bothering her. A river of tears gushed forth with the telling of the death of her son. Her eldest son had died about five years ago, and since then, she said, "my life has not been the same. I cannot stop thinking about the beautiful life he never had." As a young clinician, I was befuddled. Death of a child at any age is difficult to accept. Although I wanted to leave the room, believing I had nothing to offer this woman, I desperately wanted to help her. To bide my time while thinking about what I should do, I asked her to tell me about her life.

Slowly, in a voice that was barely audible, she began to talk about how wonderful her life was when her children were growing up. Her husband had never made a good living but was dedicated to his family and "to education." Her eldest son became a "famous lawyer" her two daughters "married educated men" and her youngest son became "a great professor." When her husband died in his fifties, it was her eldest son who "made sure that I did not want for anything." Although she was proud of her youngest son, he had taken an academic position in another city and then had married out of the faith. Her eldest son had married "a beautiful jewish girl." She then continued by comparing her eldest son to her father.

Her father had been a caretaker [a shamus] in a small synagogue when she was growing up. Although a learned man, he had little formal education, but because he liked to read the Bible and the Tamlud, he took a job that was below him. Devoted to his family, education was the most important goal for his children. She added, "He was ahead of his time. He wanted my sister and me to be as educated as my brother." She then went into great detail about how he would sit his three children on the couch and discuss with them the portion of the Old Testament that was being read that week in the synagogue. As she talked the depression lifted and she became rather animated. With a smile on her face, she imitated how he would stroke his beard when formulating a question for even the youngest of the three to answer. He would often say to her who was the youngest: "If the question is too hard my little beauty, I will ask it a little differently. And then stroking his beard, he would try to rephrase the question but it always seemed to come out even harder. And then he would laugh and say that he would save the question for next year."

As she was reconstructing her past, and obviously feeling much better, I kept thinking to myself that she had not said a word about her mother and that maybe I should ask her about her mother. Concurrently, I was terribly concerned that I had not completed my assignment to gather responses to the Rorschach. But because she was feeling better, I was feeling very conflicted. Anxious and befuddled, I was only half-listening to her reportage.

Quite suddenly she stood up and said "I feel much better now. I have an appointment." "Oh," I said, "and where is your appointment?" She retorted in a rather firm voice, "Every Thursday I have an appointment at the beauty parlor at 10:30. If I'm not there by 20 past, she knows I'm not coming. It is now 10:00 and I must get ready for my appointment." As she walked toward the door she took my arm [which I thought was inappropriate because my training was in psychodynamic therapy], and it was apparent that she wished me to walk her to the elevator. She then thanked me profusely.

My appointment with my supervisor was for a week away because it was expected that I would need some time to write up the results of the psychological testing and synthesize a written report. I was terribly anxious. Unsure of what to do, I discussed the experience with Grunes who turned the question back to me. I responded, "The only thing I learned is that if I listened to her, she felt better."

After much probing, it became apparent to me that what she needed was a benevolent person to listen to her. She was able to use me to reconstruct her past and to feel good about herself. Bolstered by the warm memories of her past life, the preoccupation with her son's death receded and she became less visibly depressed. No conflicts were resolved and no insights gained. Grunes explained that I was helpful and that if I saw her weekly, she would most likely be able to contain the depression. When he congratulated me on being such a good listener and being able to see her in the way she had been rather than only in the way she is now, I felt compelled to tell him that the reason I did not interject many questions and simply let her talk was because I kept thinking about how I was not fulfilling the assignment and was, also, preoccupied with what I should be doing. Fortunately, I was also fascinated by the process in which she seemed to become transformed while reconstructing her past. It was this fascination, as well as an ability to appreciate the ambience of intellectual curiosity created by her father, that assisted her in reconstructing the past and making herself vivid to herself.

When later I reflected on what I had learned, it seemed to me that I only needed to listen empathically to Mrs. Davis for her to recapture her earliest memories, reconstruct them in an organized and vivid manner, and thereby contain her depression. Was it this simple? Obviously, I had to be an interested listener who communicated to Mrs. Davis that she was a worthwhile person and deserved to have my attention. But, additionally, I was aware that I was letting myself visualize her as she visualized herself, particularly as she wished me to visual her as she existed in her past. When later I met with my supervisor to review the therapeutic encounter, he made an interesting observation. He said that his interest in working with the very old came, in large part, from a desire to experience as much as possible how life was for our forbearers. So too, did I realize, it is one of my motives in working with the very old.

ENHANCING MAGICAL COPING

A patient that Goldfarb often used for illustrating his inflating beliefs in mastery was a woman with crippling arthritis whose passion was knitting scarfs for her numerous grandchildren and great grandchildren. Through his encouragement, she resumed knitting, and although the scarfs were of poor quality, she was able to reestablish a sense of mastery. A similar kind of encouragement was Grunes' treatment of Miss Petosky which I have reconstructed from my memories of my earlier years in clinical training:

Miss Petosky had been a famous, and infamous, diva of an internationally renowned opera company. Now, at 92, she was a resident in the home, and all she had left were her memories. To sustain herself, Miss Petosky was writing her memoirs. Whereas the written words were unintelligible, her stories were wonderful. In her youth she had many lovers, and at one time had three lovers, all famous men, in three different cities. But she had cycles. She would go from a fulfilling immersion in writing her memoirs to becoming suicidally depressed saying, "Nobody wants to read about an old lady's life." Grunes at these times would bring his many trainees, mostly men, to Miss Petosky's room, prepping them beforehand to express adulation for Miss Petosky. This was not difficult because her stories were always interesting and filled with modestly told, but sexually revealing anecdotes. After silently reading Miss Petosky's scratchy unintelligible writing, he would put his arms around her and praise her for her excellent memoirs. Following his gestures and words, Miss Petosky's depression would lift before our eyes, and she would return to writing; that is, until the next time she became depressed.

Grunes' approach to Miss Petosky is similar to the therapeutic approach Goldfarb advocated for use with her elderly patients. Indeed, as noted initially in this chapter, the two approaches are compatible and mutually reinforcing. Both approaches were developed in nursing homes for patients in acute distress whose sense of self was severely corroded. Whereas Goldfarb chose to restore the sense of a persistent self through mastery of the external world, Grunes chose to restore the sense of a persistence self through reconstructing early life. Surely, however, for those very old persons who have lost the belief in mastery of the world and are unable to reaffirm themselves through organized, reconstructions of the past, either approach may yield generalized benefits. For these patients, regaining beliefs in mastery leads to organized reconstructions of the past and, in turn, regaining organized reconstructions of the past leads to regaining beliefs in mastery. Both reestablish a coherent, persistent sense of self and, moreover, both are ways of mobilizing passive individuals and to restoring or inculcating a beneficial kind of aggressiveness.

ACTIONS, NOT WORDS

The kinds of supportive psychotherapies proposed by Goldfarb and Grunes, the "talking cares," may not, however, always be the most appropriate for very old persons. Sometimes it is most sensible to modify the current environment; at other times, to directly modify behavior; and still at other times, to totally change the environment.

Modification of the Current Environment

An example of the modification of the current environment follows:

A competent administrator of an age-segregated housing complex presented the case of Mrs. Morrison, a quite abusive resident who was unwilling to acknowledge her need for assistance to retain her apartment. She, for example, often left on a burner on her electric stove but refused to let anyone in to see if it was left on. Only in the third session was the administrator able to accept that Mrs. Morrison's nastiness was beneficial and that it was appropriate for Mrs. Morrison to perceive an infringement on her autonomy if she entered Mrs. Morrison's apartment without her permission. By changing the times the homemaker assistant entered her apartment, the problem of intrusion was resolved. That is, Mrs. Morrison was simply informed that the homemaker assistant would continue to come in once a week for heavy cleaning but also would come in once or more every day to check out whether the apartment needed additional cleaning. These latter visits to the apartment, of course, coincided with the times Mrs. Morrison was most likely to leave on her stove, after she prepared her morning coffee and after she cooked her dinner. Congregate lunches were provided in the apartment building.

Although Mrs. Morrison will continue to be abusive, she is being protected from harming herself. She persists in being the kind of resident who is most angry when special programs are developed to accommodate those whose health is failing. They may say: "I don't want to live with those sick and crazy people! Isn't this a place for only those who can take care of themselves!" Yet when these residents, or their abusive friends, later need and participate in the program, they are likely to turn on the residents who do not want the program and vilify them: "I paid my money! This is my home! It ain't hurting you if I get something extra!"

Modification of Behavior

Another example from age segregated housing came from one of my students working in a residence for the elderly. She was concerned that her supervisor was not doing enough for a client:

Mrs. Bauer had related an incident in which she believed the door of her refrigerator had "intentionally" hit her on the back. Apparently, Mrs. Bauer had pushed the door to close it but it had not closed but rather swung back and hit her. She also was stuffing newspaper down the toilet but would not share with the student or the supervisor the reason for stuffing up the toilet. In class, the student voiced her belief that Mrs. Bauer stuffed up the toilet as a barrier to something she feared would come out of the toilet. The student's supervisor insisted that she get dressed and leave her room early in the day without attempting to discover Mrs. Bauer's paranoid fantasies. The student worker was assigned to assist in this mobilizing effort and to report on whether her paranoia subsided. The supervisor understood from experience that paranoid ideation subsides following reengagement in activities and a cessation of isolation; and, also, that extremely frightening paranoid ideation is different from the benign functional paranoia reflected in suspiciousness and distrustfulness in the absence of paranoid ideation.

The distinction was discussed in class including why some paranoia is functional, (essentially discussing content on aggressiveness and functional paranoia included in Chapter 1). Then, a few weeks later, the student reported that Mrs. Bauer began leaving her room to participate in activities and was not at all preoccupied with any paranoid ideation.

She refused to discuss the content of her former paranoid ideation, but was somewhat suspicious and distrustful. Now, however, she did communicate that the student and the supervisor had helped immensely, that their caring had helped her get better. Now that she felt protected, she no longer believed that things were coming out of the toilet to attack her, nor that she would be attached by whatever was pushing the refrigerator door. Certainly, one meaning of paranoia for the very old who have suffered losses is: "If you really cared for me, you would make it better, make me healthier and shield me from harm." Alone in her room and isolated from others, she apparently felt abandoned to all kinds of imagined dangers.

Into Protective Setting

Older people who have lived marginal lives, such as those with severe mental illness, are often best treated by placement in a protected, structured setting.

Mr. Zander was seen on the inpatient psychiatric unit as his discharge was being considered. The police brought in Mr. Zander when they found him wandering about aimlessly on the street. He said he was in a far away city looking for the house of his sister-in-law. Once in the hospital, the delusion lifted and he told the interviewer that he could have been a professor but preferred being a bookkeeper. He lived at home with his parents until his mid-forties when he was courted by a woman in her late thirties. Although reluctant to leave his parents' home, he married and was content in the marriage because his wife took such good care of him. Then, when he was 67, four years ago, she died. By now, his parents were dead and the only person to whom he could turn was his sister-in-law in the foreign city. He visited her, but she did not offer to take him in to live with her as he had hoped. When he returned to his empty apartment, he fantasized at times about visiting with his sister-in-law. Fantasy melded with reality and at times he believed he was invited to visit or actually visiting. When stopped by one policeman, he thought he was visiting her.

There was no way Mr. Zander could function without reestablishing a relationship with someone to take care of him. If taken care of, he could maintain his marginal existence. It was recommended that he move to a protective environment.

Structuring the interpersonal environment without concurrent psychotherapy is also relevant for elderly persons with cognitive impairment, as will be discussed in later chapters, particularly when working with families (Chapter 3) and in institutions (Chapter 5). Nor should behavioral therapies be overlooked (Chapter 5).

RECONSTRUCTIVE PSYCHOTHERAPY

Reconstructive, or insight, psychotherapy with the very old was impeded by Freud's admonition that older patients are too rigid to benefit from psychoanalysis. Abraham (1919) disagreed with Freud and reported the successful psychoanalysis of older patients, although "older patients" were considered to be above 50 years of age. Reports now abound of psychotherapeutic successes with patients in their seventies, eighties and even nineties. Among those who have counteracted the resistance to using insight therapies with the very old is Butler (1963), who focused on how the inevitable life review evoked by nearness to death can be used therapeutically to resolve life-long conflicts. Butler's optimism has a counterpart in Pollock's (1987) perspective of how early losses can be successfully resolved by very old persons and lead to liberation. The therapeutic process, by assisting in the liberation can awaken creativity and eventuate in dignity, self-respect and usefulness. Insight therapies are not precluded because of age. Again, it is the nature of the psychopathology and the age of the psychopathology, and not the age of the patient, that must be the first consideration.

Reconstructive psychotherapy can benefit very old persons, but there may need to be modifications in processes and outcomes. Grunes (1987), for example, argues for the need for a special kind of empathy because of psychological distance and the countertransference issues evoked. Berezin (1987) disagrees with Grunes, and cautions that the presence of limited possibilities and narcissistic depletion casts a shadow on the therapeutic encounter. Myers (1984) believes that if the capacity for insight exists (and a neurotic transference can be developed), psychodynamic therapy proceeds independent of the age of the person. Hildebrand from a personal communication, is now successfully treating a 93-year-old woman, and, according to him, no special transference issues have been evoked because of her advanced age.

Thus, there are differences among experienced clinicians in how process is modified, but there are also differences in expected outcomes. Berezin's view leads to different criteria of successful outcomes for older persons than for younger persons who have more extended futures. Hildebrand's, and certainly Pollock's, views suggest the same criteria for older and younger persons. Not considered, however, are criteria for successful reconstructive therapy that includes the normative psychological processes inherent in the unique psychology of the very old. Should a goal be to assist in making the past vivid or to overinflate beliefs in mastery? Should these processes, which are goals of Grunes' and Goldfarb's supportive psychotherapy, also be goals for reconstructive psychotherapy? The functions these processes serve for the preservation of the self of those who are very old would suggest that they should indeed be incorporated as goals.

WHAT WE DO DIFFERENTLY

Because practice wisdom is so important in informing us about counseling the aging, a systematic investigation was designed to determine whether clinicians who work with the elderly would affirm aforementioned processes and possibly add additional processes. Our approach was to ask practitioners what they do differently with older persons. Moving from practice wisdom to a systematic investigation entailed developing a set of questions that could be asked of practitioners in their practice with older persons. As will be apparent, the study was broadened to include a diversity of practitioners, administrators as well as therapists, but, for convenience, to focus only on social workers.

To be sure, each of us has our own approach to working with people. Some of us devote all or most of our time to direct treatment, others to case management, and still others to planning and administration. Also, some of us have a more psychodynamic orientation, some a humanistic, others a cognitive and still others a behavioral orientation; and some of us combine orientations into a personal eclecticism. Can we expect that despite these differences there are some commonalities in working with the aged? Possibly, these commonalities reflect shared characteristics of workers who purposively select to work with the elderly. A more likely explanation is that commonalities are a function of shared characteristics of the elderly. That is, shared characteristics among the elderly must in some way influence how we work with them in ways that are different from work with younger people.

Researchers, however, have not yet provided sufficient evidence that the content of treatment is, or should be, different. A review of the literature, as well as personal clinical experience and the clinical experience of others, led to the identification of five dimensions of potential differences: activity, touching, use of reminiscence, perceptions of the worker by the client (transference), and concerns evoked in the worker (countertransference). A study was thus undertaken to assess the validity of these dimensions. It was found that 541 respondents, subscribers to the *Journal of Gerontological Social Work*, tended to agree with the 20 statements characterizing the five dimensions (Tobin & Gustafson, 1987).

Activity

Activity of workers, as expected, was perceived to be greater with the elderly, including more coordination of services, more reaching out to difficult families, giving more concrete assistance, and more talking by the worker in sessions. The necessity for greater activity can be explained by the nature of elderly clients who are more likely to have a multiplicity of problems in which physical deficits, social losses and psychological decrements interact in a context of lessened social supports and inexperience in mobilizing formal supports. From one perspective, therefore, the problems confronting older clients are more concrete, less amenable to change and thus necessitate activity beyond the therapeutic encounter itself. Thus, case management has been advocated that encompasses developing a treatment or service plan, delivering services, and monitoring and modifying service delivery as needed. It appears, then, that it is the different needs of elderly clients that dictates the greater activity of workers.

It is possible, however, to wish to do much. Instructive is a report by child psychoanalysts Poggi and Berland (1985) on their experience in a senior citizens apartment building. To be helpful to residents, Poggi and Berland chose to provide a group experience to women in a residential setting. After the first few sessions, they became aware that they were not perceiving group members as women. When they discussed their attitudes toward participants with each other, they realized, that is, that they were desexualizing them, which certainly is unlikely to occur when psychoanalysts work with persons of other ages. They attributed their attitudes primarily to being perceived by the women as "boys" rather than as therapists; and, secondarily, to feeling a need to rescue them through providing assurance and concrete assistance. Fortunately, they corrected their misguided approach and began to perceive the elderly women as the women saw themselves, as people with persistent sexual identities despite losses. Indeed, these women, as people of any age, have a need to be perceived as possessing their sexual identities. As they began to understand that being perceived as "boys" reflected the women's attempt to retain their identities rather than as a purposeful infantilization of them, they were able to allow themselves to be perceived as "boys" without a threat to their professionalism. Moreover, they concluded, that while providing assurance and concrete assistance is important, it could not supplant facilitating the capturing of the persistent and stable self.

Touching

Touching reflects an extension of the workers' active approach to the elderly's needs. Whereas clients may not fully understand other activities of workers, touching is something that is readily understood and experienced. It is experienced as a form of caring for those who need help and assurance when in turmoil. Touching was acknowledged as a form of easily recognized caring, that they touched the elderly more, and that support is conveyed better by touching than by words. It is more, however, than a show of caring. The "laying on of hands as a form of symbolic healing" emerged in discussion with one experienced clinician struggling to understand why he, trained in psychoanalysis not to touch, did indeed touch and found it important to do so. Grunes, when teaching the meaningfulness of touching, emphasized how the elderly can feel untouchable because of bodily deterioration that makes them feel unattractive and thus unlovable.

Reminiscence

The value of reminiscence to elderly clients is, of course, not new to clinical social workers who have been taught and, also, have learned through experience, that helping clients to exploit their ego strengths and coping capacities involves discussing the ways in which successful adaptation has occurred in the past. This, too, is important in the elderly, but more specific to the elderly than for persons of other ages is the use of the past to recapture and reaffirm the current self (agreed upon by close to nine of 10 respondents). There was not much agreement, however, that having a life span makes reminiscence better suited to the elderly. The usefulness of the past, apparently, is not a function of its length per se but rather how it can be used and made vivid to maintain a constancy of the self when confronted with a loosening of a sense of identity from age-associated decrements and losses.

Transference

Transference refers to projections onto the worker of meanings, wishes and thoughts that are redirected from other persons. Although it occurs in all relationships, and presumably in exaggerated forms in helping relationships, interventions vary as to the use of transference in treatment. Independent of how, or whether, the transference is used by workers, it is not uncommon for workers to notice that the transference of older clients is somewhat different than among younger clients. Most common is for workers to observe that they are being perceived more as an authority figure. The usual explanation for this projection focuses on how the elderly have been socialized to respect authority figures, especially members of the health professions and particularly physicians (61% agreed). Beyond relating to the worker as an authority figure was the expectation that workers would perceive older people as projecting more omnipotence onto them. Respondents, however, did not perceive this as a difference (40.5%).

There are probably qualities of transference that were not captured by the survey items. For example, when helping the elderly to recapture themselves through reminiscence, the worker may feel that he or she is experienced as a person from the client's early life in a different way than occurs with younger people. It was difficult, however, for experienced clinicians to put this qualitative difference into words. This elusive transference, as well as others, certainly needs more in-depth clinical and empirical study.

Countertransference

Regarding countertransference, in much the same way that individual clients evoke projections by workers onto them, client groups with similar problems will evoke common concerns among workers. Substance abuse clients may evoke concerns with self indulgence and passivity; clients mourning death of a loved one, with concerns of losing others; and clients who have abused children or spouse, with concerns regarding potential to harm others. So too, elderly clients, because they share common situations and problems, can evoke shared concerns among workers. Based on these data, concerns regarding dependency, helplessness, death and aging of parents are the most common shared themes. In addition, some workers sometimes feel like a child when relating to elderly clients, but this feeling was not at all wide spread.

This small percentage of clinicians (about one of eight) who reported sometimes feeling like a child was surprising. I often feel like an older person's child when relating to an elderly man or woman client. Perhaps "feel like a child" suggests an infantalization that the clinicians did not feel. Recall that the child psychoanalysts Poggi and Berland, however, did feel infantalized when attempting to assist women in high rise congregate housing. Fears of infantalization may cause a withdrawal from treatment of elder persons:

At 72, Mrs. Victor who best fit the diagnosis of narcissistic character disorder, was in extreme distress. She wanted to leave her current husband, but felt herself to be "too old-looking to get another man." Yet, she was well preserved for her age, and the trainee's first impression was of a very attractive woman in her late forties or early fifties. But the trainee perceived this potential client as not amenable to treatment. In the initial diagnostic session, Mrs. Victor had referred to the trainee as "honey," "dearie," "sweetie," and other prosaic terms of endearment that made the trainee feel like a little girl. The trainee resisted the interpretation that her wish not to treat Mrs. Victor was because of feelings of being infantalized, but she continued to see Mrs. Victor under supervision.

Mrs. Victor had never stayed with a man for more than five years until she met her current husband six years ago. Having been married three times previously, she hesitated in marrying Mr. Victor, but gave in when he insisted, "It was marriage or nothing." His wealth was an added incentive. Then, in the fourth year of the marriage she got her "itch." "The romance, you know, goes after awhile and I got my itch to move on." Nothing had really changed, except Mrs. Victor has a lifelong lacunae that she fills by overly romanticized attachments that subdue the inner emptiness. The feeling of emptiness had returned, but, now perceiving herself as no longer the "beautiful girl I have always been," she feared leaving the marriage. Not unlike many others with a similar diagnosis, Mrs. Victor was a quite bright and accomplished person.

Gradually, through supervision, the trainee became aware of her resentment at being "infantalized." Her mother, she realized, used such terms of endearment to control her through infantilizations. The trainee then began to perceive Mrs. Victor as a candidate for the kind of treatment available to patients with narcissistic character disorders and began the treatment of Mrs. Victor in earnest.

Perceiving older persons as untreatable can usually be traced to transference kinds of concerns. This is indeed sad because elderly persons are treatable. Of course, it is not always easy to maintain therapeutic optimism when confronted with an elderly client or patient who has suffered from many losses and is now in acute pain. Yet Grunes and Goldfarb, and many others, have been able to do so by maintaining a belief in their therapeutic interventions. Too often, for example, clinically depressed elderly people are misperceived as intractable to therapy. Yet, depression is treatable at any age, as are other treatable mental illnesses. It is the age of the disease and not the age of the person that must be considered.

RESISTANCE TO WORK WITH THE ELDERLY

The evocation of concerns provide insight into why some workers may avoid working with the elderly. We may not all become substance abusers but we will all have (or have had) parents who will become older, frailer and more dependent. And, of course, we ourselves will all grow older. Why then do workers choose to work with the elderly? Why risk experiencing feelings of losing parents through death (and becoming an orphan) and one's own dying?

Gratifications

Obviously there are gratifications in helping the elderly, and concerns that are evoked also present opportunities to work through these concerns. Still, more must be learned about the many and specific gratifications that can accrue in working with the elderly. Clearly, part of the gratification should be a function of how work with the elderly permits the worker to be active; how caring is communicated by touching: how reminiscence by an older person provides a poignant moment of exchange in which the octogenarian seems to be transformed into a young and vital teenager or young adult: and how the projections onto worker become so personally meaningful. Also, seeing the stability that most elderly persons exhibit can be quite reassuring for their own aging.

Not Candidates for Therapy

But if those who work with older people provide more concrete assistance because old people are needy, psychotherapists may not wish to treat the elderly because they perceive them as in great need of concrete assistance and not psychotherapy. Apparently our respondents touched old people more because they perceived old people as more needy, as well as feeling that they are unattractive and unloved. Therapists may indeed be intimidated by their needs when perceiving the depletion among the old, and, as well, the impossibility of filling voids.

Elderly individuals certainly need touching because they feel so untouchable; that is, not only untouched or unloved because of loss of a life-long spouse, but also not worthy of being touched because of age-associated physical deterioration and perceived disfigurations in appearance. Touching in these circumstances should not be perceived by psychodynamically oriented practitioners as a violation of their therapeutic principles but rather as an aid to the therapeutic encounter, as a way to help the person reestablish a sense of self-worthiness. A most recent, and interesting, example of the usefulness of touching has been provided by Eaton, Mitchell-Bonair, and Friedmann (1986), who found that gentle touching of elderly institutionalized patients with organic brain syndrome improved their nutritional intake more than verbal encouragement alone.

Thus, older persons may be perceived as needing interventions other than psychotherapy, such as concrete assistance and stroking. Also inhibiting perceiving older persons as amenable to psychotherapy are feelings evoked when elderly persons reminisce. To gerontological social workers reminiscence is perceived as useful in reaffirming the self. To those, however, who fear their own aging, reminiscence may be perceived as living in the past and, moreover, a sign that life is too short and that possibilities are too limited when you are old.

Lastly, the typical countertransference issues were evident, although as noted earlier, not to the degree expected among our respondents who work with the elderly. Particularly interesting was that only 65% of the respondents agreed, "I am aware of fears of my own death." Such fears are more likely to be found among younger people (whereas old people are more concerned, generally, with disability and how they will die) and thus are most likely to be ubiquitous among our respondents. Also, apparently, the probability of having fears of becoming dependent and helpless when working with the elderly "turn off" psychotherapists. Adding to the "turning off" are issues associated with care for the therapists' own parents that are, of course, inseparable from life-long relations with parents. Given the responses of those who work with the elderly, a fear of the evocation of countertransference issues is a likely reason why therapists do not choose to work with the elderly.

SO, WHY WORK WITH OLD PEOPLE?

In turn, given the kinds of reasons for why our respondents work differently with the elderly, it may very well be that the important question we must address is: Why should anyone wish to work with the elderly? Although this question shall be left to others to address, it certainly appears that our respondents did enjoy working with the elderly and found their work to be meaningful. Possibly, the responses to the questions on reminiscence capture one aspect of the reason for working with the elderly. Not only do we obtain pleasure from the voyeuristic listening to the reconstructions of the past but, also, to the transformation of the client, when reminiscing, in becoming increasingly vivid to self, which may provide a kind of pleasure from treatment that is unique to working with the elderly. Indeed, this perspective is quite congruent with the unique psychology of the very old in which the blending of the past and the present for self definition, as well as making the past vivid to reaffirm the self, are apparently normative occurrences. In turn, assertiveness and beliefs in mastery afford to workers a sense of intellectual discovery and, also, provide ways of working with the elderly that can provide special rewards.

Chapter 3

Working with Families

In the movie, *On Golden Pond*, Norman (played by Henry Fonda), the retired professor who is one day away from his eightieth birthday, becomes disoriented in the woods behind his summer house. He panics and runs around in circles but finally arrives at the house. Breathless and with obviously frightening heart palpitations, he sits beside his wife (Katherine Hepburn) on the couch, and as he catches his breath he turns toward her and tenderly says in a voice strained with a mixture of anxiety and relief, "When I look into your face, I can be *myself* again." This moment in the movie dramatically and poignantly captures how families help us to be ourselves. Indeed, for the very old, the greater the embeddedness in family life, the more the possibility of preserving the self. Unfortunately, however, the psychological mechanisms used by very old persons to preserve their senses of self may be troublesome to family members.

Thus the chapter begins by detailing a family consultation session, which is then used to illustrate how psychological processes useful for preserving the self of a man in his nineties were sources of annoyance and concern for his offsprings who themselves were in their young-old years.

Next is a discussion of the kinds of typical feelings of family caregivers that are particularly relevant in work with families including rage from inadequacy in providing care, fears from risk-taking, frustrations associated with providers, and gratifications. A section follows on the older care receiver, particularly on emotional security gained from their family members. The chapter ends with sections on caring for Alzheimer's disease victims, practice with elderly individuals and their families during the process of becoming institutionalized, and a final comment on who is the client in work with families.

AN ILLUSTRATION OF FAMILY DYNAMICS

Details from a consultation session with a family will be used to illustrate how complaints are elicited by behaviors that are functional for persons in advanced old age:

I was asked by Jane, the granddaughter of a couple in their nineties, to meet with her, her father Joe, her mother Beth, and her father's sister Aunt Sue to consult on the caregiving arrangements for her grandparents. Jane said that her father Joe was becoming quite anxious about the caregiving arrangements. His sister, her Aunt Sue, was the primary caregiver to his parents who had decided to remain for the winter in their summer home so that Aunt Sue, who was living in the home, could provide care to them. Nothing dramatic had occurred, but father Joe feared that his sister Sue may become "burned out."

My meeting with Jane, father Joe, Mother Beth and Aunt Sue began with father Joe encouraging Aunt Sue to voice her complaints about her father. His request of Aunt Sue, said in a rather quiet voice but with an unmistakenly sarcastic tone, was something like, "Tell Dr. Tobin all those things that bother you about dad, the kinds of things you always tell me about." He then added in an aside to me that was loud enough for all to hear, "Sue said that she did not want to attend this family meeting because she gets so angry and that's not good for her."

So Aunt Sue began her litany of complaints, "Our father expects me to do everything for him and he doesn't appreciate anything I do. He never appreciated anything mother did for him and now he doesn't appreciate what I do for him. And he yells at me. At times he even thinks that I'm trying to hurt him. It's hard to take."

As if embarrassed by her anger, Aunt Sue stopped and lowered her head. Father Joe, however, encouraged her to continue, "What about his overdoing?" So Aunt Sue continued. One day, she related, he tried to carry some firewood into the house which he could not do and this activity frightened her. When she tried to discuss with him this kind of harmful behavior, he discussed how capably he built up a large business, that he still had all his faculties, that he wished to do things for himself and that it was none of her business. His constant allusions to, and embellished stories about, his great success as a businessman, she felt, was purposely used to irk her because she had married a man who tried to emulate her father but was unsuccessful in business. Eventually he took to drink and they were divorced.

Mother Beth redirected the focus toward Joe's recent anxiety. Joe, however, could not verbalize why he had become anxious. Daughter Jane, then said that it might be because he was considering slowing down now that he was close to sixty five. "No," said Joe "I have been slowing down and the business is in good shape." "How," asked Beth, "do you feel now that dad does not come into the office everyday?" This was the first autumn that his father had not come into the office for at least one hour each day. "Good and bad," said Joe "because I like seeing dad up and about, but in the last few years he hasn't really understood the direction of the company. And frankly, he thinks he does, but I don't have the heart to tell him anything different. It is especially difficult when he acts suspicious, like I'm not telling him the truth." Beth then said, "I have sensed that you have been somewhat relieved that the old man isn't there to tell you how he built up the business and ignore all that you have done to keep it going." Joe responded, "After forty years, you learn to accept that."

The conversation stopped, and everyone turned to me. I asked "What about grandma?" All agreed that grandpa would not have been successful had not grandma been there to encourage and support his ventures. She was his sounding board and all chuckled when reminiscing about how her sense of business was probably better than grandpa's.

Then, rather suddenly the precipitant for the session was brought out. Every year grandpa goes into the hospital for an annual checkup. During the week he is away, grandma uses the time away from her spouse of over seventy years to visit one of her three daughters. This year, however, she said that she was too frail and did not want to bother her daughters or to be among vigorous noisy grandchildren. Instead she was thinking of going into the hospital herself for a complete checkup. This thought of grandma's frightened Aunt Sue, as well as father Joe, because their mother has always insulated them from their father. Also they were aware and frightened of her increasing frailty.

Joe, who was now fidgeting, suddenly sprang up and said that he needed to go to the bathroom and to get a cup of coffee. It was now one hour into a session that lasted for more than two hours. A break seemed sensible. When we all returned to our chairs, Joe was sweating and his face was ashen. What was wrong? After a few minutes of silence, Beth said something to the effect "So that's what its all about Joe. You are still mama's little boy and the thought of mama not being there to help you with dad is the problem."

In a low and strained voice, Joe began by denying that this was the problem. But then his daughter Jane said very directly that the purpose of this session was to obtain guidance and that indeed it was the change in his mother that was bothering him, that he should share his feelings with us. With an apparent sigh of relief, he began to talk about his mother. Whenever he decided upon a new direction for the business, he first went to his mother, as did his father. If she agreed his decision was a wise or sensible one, than she gently convinced her husband that he should accept his son's judgment. What often happened, however, was that his father took the decision as his own without giving any credit to his son. For Joe, it was only his mother who truly understood his importance. Without her, there would be no one who understood how much of a man he had become and that he no longer walked in the shadow of his father.

It was a sad moment for Joe but also one in which support could be given to him. His wife, sister, and daughter assured him in no uncertain terms that they were aware of what he had contributed. After reviewing some of the important decisions he had made, Mother Beth lightened the air by saying "Maybe now you can slow down and we can go some long vacations. We have to spend the money you made some way." Turning to Aunt Sue, Mother Beth asked if their going away would be a hardship because they would not be available if there was a crisis. Now very thoughtfully Aunt Sue replied, "I'm always scared something will happen. I can't enjoy myself. You go away."

There was never a second session. I left it to Jane to contact me if the family wished to continue or if Joe, by himself, wished to be seen in counseling. About two months later, Jane told me that the situation remained stable with Aunt Sue continuing to complain angrily and vociferously, but enjoying being the "special and best child."

The lengthy single session with this family certainly revealed the kinds of complaints found among caregivers in response to behaviors that preserve the self. It also revealed the persistence of family psychodynamics and, fortunately, how lifelong dysfunctional psychodynamics can be made manifest and begun to be worked through. Joe was able to use this session to begin to free himself from a preoccupation that has been very troublesome for him.

COMPLAINTS ABOUT FUNCTIONAL BEHAVIORS

Aunt Sue, as well as father Joe, indeed complained about behaviors that are helpful to grandpa, behaviors encompassed under the unique psychology of the very old: a nasty aggressiveness, magical coping, and repetitive, vivid reminiscence. And they also complained that grandpa is still himself.

Aggressiveness

Grandpa was always feisty. His determination led him to build an enormously successful business and to make himself a millionaire several times over. But he was not known to be a particularly distrustful or suspicious person. Yet now Joe is concerned that his father "acts suspicious, like I'm not telling the truth." Aunt Sue not only concurs but augments this impression, "At times he even thinks I'm going to hurt him." The concerns are about grandpa's functional paranoia, distrust and suspicion which is unaccompanied by anything as serious as delusions of persecution. Still, the attacks on them by their father are hard to take.

As a member of a support group for family caregivers said of her impaired father, "What I do for him is never enough and, you can bet, he always tells me so." Another said, "He keeps telling me what I do that is wrong." And still another, "I don't mind if she doesn't trust anybody else. But I take care of her. And I do the best I can." It may be best for the homebound mother who lives with her caregiving daughter to externalize her anger toward her plight, but it certainly is not best for the daughter onto whom the rage is displaced, especially when the beleaguered daughter is devoting many hours to caring for her mother and taking much time away from her husband and children.

Magical Coping

Magical coping, also evident in grandpa's behavior, is a cause of concern. As portrayed by Aunt Sue, he tries to participate in some of the physical activities that assure him of his manliness such as carrying firewood into the house. Joe, however, is disturbed by his father's beliefs that he understands the company as it now is. Fortunately, Joe is sufficiently sensitive to his father's needs that he does not confront him with the unreality of his beneficial illusions.

Most caregivers have concerns about magical coping, particularly when the elderly family member is doing something that may be harmful. "She can't see anymore to cook but there she is turning on the stove. She will catch on fire. She wears this inflammable night gown to cook her breakfast." Or "He doesn't know how dangerous he is to himself." Often have I heard, "She doesn't know that she can't take care of herself anymore."

A secretary who worked half-time, as did her sister, so that they could share caregiving for their homebound mother, told of her frustration after typing one of my articles: "This is my mother! She thinks she can do everything she ever did. She walks around all day long turning off the radiators because she feels overheated. She doesn't have the strength to turn the knob. It doesn't do any good to tell her. But one of these days she is going to fall down and break a leg or a hip and then I will really be in trouble. It's hard enough to care for her now!"

Repetitive Reminiscence

Hurtful to Aunt Sue is her father's incessant talking about how he built his business. These reminiscences, which are a source of great self-esteem to her father, are disturbing to Aunt Sue particularly because of how she interprets them. In the telling of his great successes, her father is perceived as putting her down because of her marriage to an unsuccessful businessman. The content of the discussion during the consultation session, however, suggests that grandpa was not the least bit interested in Aunt Sue's long forgotten divorce but, rather, interested in recalling his business success when now he was no longer the prominent businessman he once had been.

Others also complaining about repetitive reminiscence, "I'm going to bring someone in to tell his stories to. At least three times a day he tells me about growing up in the old country." Or, "Whenever we have a conversation we never finish it because she starts to tell stories about the good old days." "How often" said the distraught daughter "must I hear the same old stories of how my dad struggled to feed us in the Depression. Sure, he is trying to say that my helping him now is only paying him back for what he did for us. When I try to tell him I would do for him anyway and that he should read the paper like he used to so we have something to talk about, two minutes later he is back talking about how we starved but made it."

Persistent Family Dynamics

As a listener at the family session I was very impressed with how grandpa has been able to be himself through his mid-nineties. He, apparently, is as arrogant as ever and as unwilling as ever to give credit to anybody including his wife who is seen by her children as the real wise one in the family. It is the persistence of grandpa's identity which makes Aunt Sue most uncomfortable because it is a constant reminder of her failure in finding a suitable mate; for her, a mate acceptable to her father. Grandpa, in being himself, is also a reminder to his son Joe that he should not feel so successful because he took over a thriving business built by his father. Fortunately, at 65 Joe is beginning to reject this internalized evaluation of his father. Thus the session not only revealed the kinds of complaints found among caregivers about psychological mechanisms useful for preservation of the self, but also the persistence of family psychodynamics.

Caregiving family members often complain about how parents say things that trigger off life-long sensitive issues such as "Papa really knows what to say that hurts me!" or "Mama always compares me to my sister who was always favored!" Each person in their old-old years, in trying to be themselves, will attempt to play out their life-long relationships with their children. But it certainly is difficult for caregivers when characteristic ways of interacting trigger off underlying resentments and conflicts. Because of the persistence of these psychodynamics in the relationship, it is erroneous to consider a "role reversal" in which the parent who was once the caregiver is now the care receiver. Family interaction is always characterized by interdependence, a complex mixture of dependence and independence among members. Of course, there are differences. Caring for an infant contains the anticipation of a rewarding future of growth and development whereas caring for a debilitated parent contains a downward course followed by death. And older people are likely to provide more monetary assistance to adult children than their children provide to them. It is, however, the persistence of psychodynamics that is most characteristic of caring relationships among the very old and it is this very persistence, albeit a disturbance to caregivers, that helps in the preservation of the self.

Bumagin, a gerontological social worker, illustrates this persistence when telling of the daughter who was giving her incontinent mother a sponge bath. Mother, in a prone position looked up at her disheveled daughter and said "I always liked you in red." Mother, with her chatter about clothes and appearances, redefined the moment to maintain a persistent relationship. The daughter, who has a sister who the mother has always thought was prettier, winces, bites her tongue and tries to continue to be gentle.

FEELINGS OF FAMILY CAREGIVERS

The more that feelings of family caregivers are understood, the more it becomes possible to help them to continue to contribute to the emotional well-being, as well as to the preservation of self, of their impaired member. For example, the complaints about behaviors that are beneficial to care receivers are often only the tip of the iceberg. Below the surface, and sometimes just below, may be rage, a rage that is likely to be evoked by feelings toward the family member for whom care is being provided for causing feelings of inadequacy. Some other feelings of caregiving family members of which workers must be aware are the fears when risks are taken, the guilt of taking time away from other members of the family, the frustrations in relating to providers, and also the gratifications. Feelings are indeed many, complex and usually quite ambivalent.

Underlying Rage

Feelings of inadequacy when giving care are generated by a desire, often unconscious but rather unavoidable, to make the recipient of care healthy again. Aunt Sue was able to express some of her feelings of inadequacy when she communicated that she could not vacation away from her parents because she carries around this feeling of having to be with them when an inevitable crisis occurs. Her feeling is less of guilt regarding what she is not doing for her parents and more of impotence, of not being able to do anything that will keep them healthy. For Aunt Sue, these feelings are fused with her feelings of being angry, possibly enraged, for not being sufficiently appreciated for the dedication to caring and for having her defenses penetrated with a consequent resurrecting of painful inner experiences left over from her earlier years.

Fears from Risk Taking

Aunt Sue was not providing the kind of care that causes great fears in risk taking. Hasselkuss (1988), from in-depth interviews with caregivers, identified this fear as a major theme:

> A fear of change, or anything which might cause a change, was usually present. "Now he's got a sore on the other foot, so now I'm worried about that one." Activities were governed by their perceived safety ("We planned to stay longer [vacation], but the glucose count started to go up and we just felt uncomfortable—we'd had so many frightening things happen—so we came home"). Some care procedures were perceived as risky ("We used a condom catheter when he first came home; you were always afraid of getting that too tight"). Risk associated with leaving the care receiver home alone was sometimes handled by putting the care receiver to bed during the caregiver's absence. "Oh, I wouldn't leave him in the wheelchair, he gets into things. He loves to smoke and I don't trust him, he'd burn up, so he's better off in bed." (p. 688).

Deserting Others

It is not uncommon for caregiving middle aged children to feel guilty about taking time away from others. Deserting others was found by doctoral student Smith (1988, personal communication) to be a dominant theme in counseling in Professor Ronald Toseland's project, which focused on comparing the effectiveness in reducing caregiver's strain by professionals and by peers in support groups and in individual counseling. Smith, then a doctoral student, was one of the professional counselors, and she also supervised and monitored professionals and peers who provided individual counseling to the middle aged female caregivers.

Smith observed that many who are caring for elderly parents felt they were neglecting their spouse, that they lost their privacy and at times their intimacy with their husband, and that their marriage was under a great deal of stress. Some used much energy to shelter their husband from feeling any burden or responsibility for the care of the frail elderly parent. One woman said, "My husband is a wonderful, patient man, I don't want to burden him with any responsibilities regarding the care of our parent." Another commented, "I don't like to complain to my husband. It just gets him angry. He doesn't understand why I can't get others to help with mom." Few women felt that their husbands understood them, nor that they would actually help them. Most were fearful that their husbands would just get more angry, become more sullen or withdrawn, or insist on nursing home placement if they were asked to assume more caregiving responsibilities. It was the impression of counselors that those marriages presently very stormy were likely to have been shaky before caregiving. Whereas, to be sure, caregiving puts an added stress on relationships, mutually supportive relationships tend to survive these stresses better than insecure, unhappy relationships. During counseling, concerns about marital relationships were discussed to alleviate conflict.

Parent-child issues were present with some of the caregivers but not as prevalent as marital problems. Caregivers felt that their parent-child problems were present because of the stages their children were going through. Yet, these adult daughters felt they could, and did, mobilize their children into sharing some of the daily chores regarding care of their grandparents. There was a sense of control felt by the women over their children which was not present with their spouses.

Relationships between siblings was also a major topic of discussion which encompassed siblings of the caregiver, as well as siblings of the care receiver. The primary caregiver often felt stuck in her role and had difficulty thinking how she could effectively mobilize others into the role of caregiving. Letting siblings know how she felt and what kinds of help she would appreciate was something that was worked on regularly during the counseling sessions. Statements such as the following were made by the clients. "I know I chose this role. It is my problem now." I don't want to appear that I can't handle Mom." "I don't want to sound like a cry baby." "My brother has his own problems. What good would it do to burden him with more problems?" "They live so far away. Why

tell them what it's really like for me? They can't do anything, anyways."
These and similar statements were made regularly by the caregivers.
Help was given to the clients in sharing some of their burden and feel-
ings with other family members, as was provided to Aunt Sue.

Frustrations Related to Providers

A recurrent theme in counseling is frustrations related to providers. The
most frequent complaint was to find and keep qualified, competent,
and reliable home health aides. Fear of rejection by aides was a major
problem that caregivers often verbalized. Daughters often felt at the
mercy of these employees and felt powerless to do anything to change
the situation. Assistance was, however, provided in counseling sessions
as caregivers learned how to relate to aides in different ways, how to
make better use to them, how to make their jobs a little more interesting, and how to reward the aides with appropriate praise and encouragement. Other concerns were associated with a lack of information
regarding existing services, as well as a lack of knowledge of how to ac-
cess them.

Hasselkuss (1988), however, identified a theme of tensions with professionals rather than aides as Smith reported. One of Hasselkuss' respondents commented, "The occupational therapist wanted to come
early and watch me, what I did and everything, and it made me so
nervous. So I asked the occupational therapist not to come anymore"
(p. 688). Also noted were tensions among caregivers, care receivers and
professionals. At times caregivers commented that health professionals
made remarks that undermined caregiver's efforts. A caregiver reported
that the nurse chided her for feeding the care receiver greasy potato
pancakes that could "close an artery and clog it, that he wasn't getting
enough blood to the brain."

It is quite understandable why Smith found that caregivers often do
not feel in control and need to exert too much control, particularly when
unacceptable feelings of rage are provoked by care receivers' behaviors.
As noted by Smith (1988, personal communication):

> Sometime children who are caregivers are unaware that their anger relates
> to how the care receiver makes them feel inadequate. As an outside ob-
> server, it is certainly understandable that a caregiver would feel toward a
> parent for whom they are providing care that the parent has placed him
> or her in an intolerable position. The frail elderly care receiver has become
> the source for feelings of inadequacy, as well as for raising issues that re-
> late back to childhood that have been repressed for a lifetime. A common

way to deal with some of these less conscious feelings is to focus the anger on specific behaviors. The caregiving child becomes angry at, for example, suspicious or paranoid behavior that all too often makes caregiving extremely difficult. The paradox is, of course, that the projection of blame for disability by the elderly family caregiver onto others is very functional. Once again, when internal deterioration occurs it is best to blame others rather than oneself.

Gratification

Aunt Sue, of course, does not only have negative feelings. She also has feelings that she is a good child and, moreover, a better child than her sibling Joe who has not, as she has, assumed the responsibilities for caring for their parents. Fortunately, usually the gratifications from caregiving outweigh the felt burdens. Because of the gratifications families receive from caring for an impaired member regardless of age, it makes it easier to let caregivers express those negative feelings that may be bottled up.

The opportunity to verbalize feelings in a support group is particularly helpful. Although the negative feelings toward care receivers can be dangerous to the holder, most caregivers can, when made conscious of them, deal with them. For most caregivers it comes as a relief that others have similar feelings and are not overwhelmed by them. In one group of family caregivers, when a daughter who was providing care to her mother mentioned her frustration and anger, another member of the group who was providing home care to her father blurted out, "I get so angry with him that there are times when I just want to kill him!" She was, fortunately, ready to deal with these feelings of great frustration and anger. In listening to others it became apparent to her that she was not alone in having these feelings and, more importantly, that she was doing an excellent job of giving care while maintaining control over her feelings. She learned that just being there, the day-to-day face-to-face contact, was of the most importance. Also she learned, as she must, what it is possible to do and what it is impossible to do.

Being a Moral Person

As noted by Smith, "These women frequency reaffirmed the morality of their decision to be caregivers, believing they were superior to others who relinquished responsibility when they placed their parents in nursing homes." Feelings of being a moral person, of fulfilling family obligations that transcend conflicts in relationships, accounts for the great extent of family caregiving. Indeed, the ties that bind families together are no greater in evidence than when care is needed by elderly members. Although about 5% of all the elderly are in nursing homes at any one time, possibly as many as three times this percentage of the elderly whose physical and mental status is comparable to those in nursing homes are being cared for in their own homes. Weissert's (1985) estimate is 12.4%. Indeed, 6% to 8% of those 65 and over may be home bound and about 3% bedridden; added to the 6% to 8% are those elderly persons who can leave their homes but need care, protection, and surveillance to do so.

RECEIVING EMOTIONAL SUPPORT

It is thus obvious that care at home rather than in a congregate setting enhances the retention of self. To be explored briefly is the emotional security from families before home care is warranted.

Before Caregiving

Studies with Kulys (see, for example, Kulys & Tobin, 1980) replicated what others have found; that less than 10% of persons 65 and over report being concerned about the future. Because, obviously, age-associated losses are going to occur, it has been easy to interpret the lack of future concern among the more than 90% as reflecting denial, an unwillingness to face the future. We found, however, that those who are not worried are not only those least likely to use denial, but are also the least anxious and depressed and, moreover, have the greatest amount of familial supports. Because of event uncertainty and the uncertainty of timing of events ("anything can happen at anytime"), to worry about what will happen is actually to be preoccupied; and it is the presence and availability of family that reduces preoccupations and permits the elderly to use present interaction for preservation of the self.

To further explore the role of family in the process of self-preservation, the person designated by respondents as their "responsible other" was also interviewed. To identify responsible others, respondents were asked: "If you were admitted to the hospital and had to name someone who would be responsible for you and your affairs, whom would you choose?" As others have found, there is a principle of substitution so that the first person named, if available, was a spouse; if unavailable, a child was named; and if neither a spouse nor a child was available, other family members were named, usually a sibling. Only when spouses, children and other family members were unavailable, were friends named.

For the 50 dyads composed of parents and children, feelings of security among parents was related to their ability to say that responsible children would take their wishes into account if decisions needed to be made for future care (Schlesinger, Tobin, & Kulys, 1981). Paradoxically, greater amounts of interaction between parent and child were associated with lessened feelings of security which, however, becomes quite understandable because increased interaction occurs when adverse events cause both lessened security and greater need for attention by children.

Knowledge of Services

Most associated with feelings of security of parents was the extent of personal care services of which responsible children had knowledge. Apparently, knowledge of concrete services by children provides the necessary reassurance that meaningful concern will be given, a kind of concern that reassures parents that they will, for example, be able to use community services to stay at home. This reassurance suggests once again that what is most meaningful to the elderly person is that the maintenance and retention of self will persist. Although there are conflicts in the parent-child relationship, when formal services are known by the child and this knowledge communicated to the parent feelings of security are enhanced.

Children Described Clearer

Each parent and responsible child was asked to describe him or herself and also to describe the other as they think the other would describe him or herself. The parent was better able to describe the child as the child described self than was the child able to describe the parent as the parent described self. One interpretation of this finding is that it is very important for parents to have a clear picture of children that are likely to be responsible for their future care. Yet, also evident in the data was the portrayal by parents of negative aspects of self that children seem to feel would not be used in parents' self-descriptions. The acceptance of previously unacceptable motives and self-perceptions is a common phenomenon among the elderly, as was noted in the first chapter. As discussed there, if the central task in advanced old age is to be oneself, then previously unacceptable thoughts and feelings become open to consciousness if they serve to preserve the self.

Spouses and Children as Caregivers

Concerns of spouses may be quite different than the concerns of children. Spouses tend to feel less ambivalent about providing care than do children and say: "He (or she) would take care of me if I needed care." Husbands, however, experience less strain because, apparently, they focus more on instrumental assistance than emotional support, which is certainly easier to provide to a frail and failing spouse who may also have Alzheimer's disease. Yet the sense of capacity experienced by husbands and wives does not ameliorate the strain from the instrumental tasks of providing assistance that may indeed be a taxing burden on spouses who themselves may be in their eighties and even nineties. Also, the emotional strain must certainly be enormous for spouses who are witnessing the deterioration of a lifelong mate. An obvious concern, therefore, is with relief from the incessant burdens of caregiving, as well as how to obtain supportive services. Also, the caregiving spouse cannot help but ask: "What will happen next?" Most painful is the thought of having to place a mate in a nursing home. Even when others, such as the family physician, say "It's time," the spouse may become quite agitated and upset. It is likely that the wife who is providing care will have feelings such as "He would never let this happen to me."

The concerns of children include those of caregiving spouses, but because of the absence of the reciprocity of marital relationships, concerns may be rather different. Often, for example, it is the very daughter who has felt most unloved who assumes the burden of caregiving as a means of gaining a feeling of being loved. For this child, caring for a parent often becomes a vehicle of discharging hostility toward siblings, as when the caregiving daughter verbalized to her sister something like, "I care more for mother than you do." Regardless of whether the caregiver feels herself to be an unloved or a loved daughter, it is often the unstated, or less conscious emotions, that cause difficulty. One such often preconscious feeling is generated when the adult child is giving care to a widowed parent where the thought of losing a second parent (and becoming an orphan) can be very frightening. The cared-for parent represents the patina between the child and his or her maker. Although not verbalized, preoccupations with one's own death are evoked. Concerns and preoccupations with dying are indeed concerns of caregivers in their middle years.

WHEN CARING FOR AN ALZHEIMER'S VICTIM

Walter Lyons (1982), a caseworker and administrator in the Bay Crest Home for the Aged in Toronto, reported on his frustrating experiences caring for his wife who was afflicted with Alzheimer's disease. Because of his background, he understood not only some of the principles in providing care but also his wife's internal feelings. He wrote the following as if these words were hers: "You only know me from the outside, through my 'abnormal behavior.' Will you see me inside, struggling to maintain my assaulted personhood? Will you mistake my struggle to retain some dignity, some feeling of self, for organic disease rather than its consequences?" (p. 3).

Retaining the Self

The struggle to retain the self among those with Alzheimer's disease is observed not only by family members but also by practitioners. Cohen and Eisdorfer (1986) titled their book on family caring for Alzheimer's disease patients, *The Loss of Self*. They begin their book with quotes from the diary of James Thomas, an Alzheimer's victim: "Help me to be strong and free until my self no longer exists" (p. 21) and "Most people expect to die some day, but who ever expected to lose their self first" (p. 22). The dissolution of the self is catastrophic for the person who is aware of the dissolution in him or herself. Apparently, a similar process occurs in the early stage of schizophrenia when the victim of this disease becomes aware that inner mental processes are becoming destructured. Indeed, the early paranoid ideation in schizophrenia may be a way of coping with this awareness in the same way that similar ideation may be a way of coping with the early awareness of Alzheimer's disease. Other parallels are that both diseases have no known cause or cure, and both are insidious because both diseases follow a course of slow and progressive deterioration. Cause for concern exists when the older person exhibits unusual changes in mental abilities that persist and become progressively worse, disrupting life routines and accompanied by unfamiliar or bizarre changes in emotional expression.

Only in later stages is the full-blown syndrome of Alzheimer's disease apparent thereby permitting a rather definitive diagnosis. Still, families must know the Senile Dementia of the Alzheimer's Type (SDAT) can only be diagnosed with finality at autopsy. To obtain a provisional diagnosis in early stages, all other possible causes for confusion and personality changes must be ruled out. Unfortunately, this is not always done, and too often elderly individuals are labelled with, and then treated as if they have, Alzheimer's disease, and with dire consequences. Necessary, and not too difficult, is to rule out some forgetfulness that may be common in advancing age; nor is it very difficult, particularly if an informant is available, to rule out confusional states that begin more suddenly and are not insidious in nature.

Many elderly who become confused indeed do not have Alzheimer's disease but rather have transient confusion from physiological or psychological causes. Physiological causes include drug effects (from the pocketbook polypharmacy), inadequate nutrition, decompensating cardiovascular and respiratory disease, and even from infections and fecal impaction, as well as visual and hearing losses that reduce comprehension causing a "false" or "pseudodementia."

Psychological causes include social dislocation, anxiety states, and depression, which is the most common cause of "pseudodementia." The older person who is depressed is really not confused ("demented") but rather indifferent to time and place. Interpreting indifference as an inability to become oriented can lead to medicating the person eventuating in a persistent confusional state. This unfortunately, is not at all rare in hospitals when busy nursing and house staff, who have never before observed the patient, interpret a lack of orientation to time and place as Alzheimer's disease. Elderly patients who are agitatedly depressed are particularly likely to suffer from this kind of iatrogenesis, as will be discussed in the next chapter on psychological distress induced in hospitalizations.

When all other causes have been ruled out and the elderly person is diagnosed as having Alzheimer's disease, a lengthy period of deterioration begins. A deselfing process has started that leads to a person who is no longer him or herself. The essential task for this family is the same as it is for families of all the elderly; that is, to help the patient be herself or himself as much as possible. Lyons (1982), after noting his wife's struggle to retain "some feeling of self," continued to describe her thoughts:

For me, this is a life and death struggle from which I can collapse into crushing defeat and withdrawal, or I can be aroused to a fever pitch of agitation and frustration expressed in pacing, in tearing at my clothing, repetitive movements or sounds. You may think I am "completely out of it," but if you watch me closely I may startle you with my awareness of, for example, the danger of walking down steps or the presence of a person, or I may be searching for a person or an activity which I usually do around this time of day. My attempts to indicate to you that I am missing something may not make sense, and you may write off my behavior as the meaningless actions of a person who lacks memory and does not know what time it is, or where he is. Yet, inside, in my own perception of things, I am reaching for something very real, and trying in my own way to find it or to get you to help me.

You may fail to help me do what I can do, by not taking the time and trouble to discover this. It is much simpler to do things for me, because that way is quicker and surer and more efficient. But, do you realize that this may make me more confused, frustrated, sometimes resistive and resentful. Sure, I am cognitively impaired, but that means you have to use your ingenuity and your patience to help me to clue into what you want me to do and try to understand what I want to do.

Then I face the opposite kind of problem, in which, because of my inability, you may think I lack motivation, and therefore you try to pull or push me into doing things in the belief that somehow, if I am not pushed into them and I am not engaged, you are colluding in making me more helpless.

But it is not only your misperceptions of me which add to my problems. It is also what you are feeling deep inside of you, because I know you are terrified by my losses. You are well-meaning, good intentioned normally kind and considerate. But inside, you cannot help but feel not just pity, but some revulsion; not just empathy but also some rejection.

When I am incontinent, I do not like it. I can still experience shame and embarrassment. But I am helpless to protect myself against it, especially when you are not tuned into my signals when I want to go. I am also helpless to protect myself against your annoyance and disgust. Do you know how dependent I am upon you to protect my dignity which is so often assaulted?

I know that you really cannot cut down all the barriers that isolate me. But you can look for those things which reduce my frustration, which help smooth the way in the face of what confounds me, if you take the time and make the effort to help me bridge, at least partially, the cognitive gap which separates me from our reality. I am not gone. I am here.

Do you really know how terribly alone I am, closed in and cut off from so many people and so many things around me? How I try, and why I cry? For God's sake, help me in my terrible isolation. That is my cry and my pain at its most raw and elemental level (pp. 3–6).

Assistance in Retaining the Self

A more poignant description of what it is to be a victim of Alzheimer's disease has not been written. Most essential to Lyons was providing assistance to his wife in being the same person, helping her to do the same things she has always done. Yet not all family caregivers are as aware as Lyons that seemingly bizarre and aimless activities are purposeful. For example, regarding the common and annoying behavior of wandering, one group (Snyder et al., 1978) identified three motives among wanderers in a nursing home: release of tension by using a lifelong pattern of coping with stress such as taking a brisk walk or a long stroll, carrying out a work role, and searching for security ("Where is my mother?").

How can families be assisted to help the Alzheimer's victim retain a sense of self? Just as Lyons learned that his wife was struggling to be herself, family members must learn that bizarre behaviors often have meanings related to the striving for preservation of self. Once this principle is understood by family members, it becomes increasingly possible for them to understand the continuity between current bizarre behavior and pre-morbid personality traits. In turn, as the bizarre behaviors become intelligible, they can tolerate, or even encourage, aberrant behaviors that help the patient still be him or herself.

Wandering is obviously not the only behavior that contains continuity with the past. Shomaker (1987) identified three additional kinds of behaviors that families of Alzheimer's victims reported as particularly disturbing to them: expression of emotions that are exaggerated or inappropriate; a lack of personal hygiene; and unintelligible communication. Yet, all these behaviors can often be understood. Men who wander may be going to their jobs; women to the grocery store. The father with Alzheimer's disease who has difficulty communicating but has sufficient cognitive abilities to follow simple conversations will naturally become enraged when the family tactlessly discusses his child-like behavior in front of him. The mother who has always been fastidious in her appearance, may scatter all her clothes on the floor while searching for a favorite brooch from her teenage years. When mother talks to her long dead mother as if she is alive and in the room, it is certainly abnormal, but it is also a seeking for security and an expression of her life-long identity.

Mother or father may not be the "same person," but she or he is still a person and in many ways is the same person. The extent to which the Alzheimer's victim feels like the same person he or she has always been, no matter how bizarre the behavior, must be accepted as the patient's reality. The distortions, that are so very painful to family members as they watch a loved one lose contact with the here and now, may indeed serve the patient's purpose of retaining a sense of self while providing assurance as the disease follows in its inexorable course.

An Inappropriate Response

An example of an inappropriate response to a family member who was a victim of the disease occurred when a husband tied his wife to a chair while he cooked the meals. When she refused to talk to him after he began to restrain her, the husband and home care worker became alarmed because their relationship had immediately deteriorated. To the worker and the husband, however, restraints made sense because his wife had previously not allowed him to prepare food in *her* kitchen. He did not object to adopting the role and responsibilities of "housewife," but he did object to her incessant interference. He only tied her down after he had frequently and painstakingly explained why she should not interfere. She would "shadow" him by standing at his elbow whenever he was in the kitchen and her interference turned the kitchen into a complete mess. Now he felt that she was being unduly angry at him for taking a necessary step. I suggested to the worker that the husband allow his wife to have the use of the kitchen, that he use a space for meal preparation that she did not ordinarily use, and to call me if he believed that the restraints continued to be needed. The worker has not called back, hopefully because his wife was not tied down and that although the kitchen was more messy, the wife talked to her husband and life was calmer.

Inability to Differentiate Thoughts and Actions

Too often, overwhelmed spouses and children of Alzheimer's victims interpret behaviors as motivated by vindictiveness as had occurred in the previous case. At other times, behavior is interpreted as lying, the purposeful telling of untruths. Being bewildered by strange behaviors when caregiving can indeed lead to perceiving the care receiver as doing spiteful things which, unfortunately, can be a projection of one's own frustrations and angry feelings. When a daughter asks her confused mother who has disheveled hair, to comb her hair and her mother answers that she just did, the mother is not "lying." Rather, it is because of her inability to differentiate between thoughts and actions. Her transient thought of hair combing becomes the belief that she did so. Zarit et al. (1985) provide many examples in addition to "lying" that are caused by not understanding the effects of memory loss. Repetitive questions are misinterpreted as a wish to be annoying or attract attention and thus, "He should control himself." This behavior more likely reflects an inability to remember asking the question or the loss of appropriate skills to gain attention. Or the family may say that she is denying her memory loss when she cannot remember. Too often explanations for behaviors that are plausible to families are not at all accurate. Above all, most beneficial to both the patient and the family, and having a calming effect on both, is acceptance.

Self-help groups have been found to be helpful. Whereas previously it was thought that families become increasingly unable to withstand the mental deterioration, Zarit et al. (1985) have reported that family caregivers in support groups report less experience of burden over time although the physical burden may be appreciably greater (e.g., Mace & Rabins, 1981, *The 36-Hour Day*). This counterintuitive finding, apparently relates to how the most trying times are when the victim and the family first become aware of the disease and, also, the subsequent phase when the deselfing process causes a marked deterioration from the premorbid state. The shift that later occurs from a moderate or extreme nonresemblence of self to a total nonresemblence is easier to accept, probably because family members have already begun to successfully mourn the loss of the identity of the person.

Responding to Bizarre Behavior

The goals of practice according to (Zarit et al., 1985) are, therefore, to differentiate irreversible dementia (SDAT) from treatable problems, to provide direct assistance to the victim in maintaining competencies and self esteem, and to help family caregivers. To emphasize again, when caregivers can respond appropriately to seemingly bizarre behavior, the victim will be helped. Zarit et al. (1985) provide a specific example:

> Mr. Pine cared for his wife, who had shown dementia symptoms for six years. One of the problems that bothered him most was that she accused him of stealing money from her purse, which he was not doing. When this happened, he would try to reason with her, but she would argue, insisting that he had taken it. The situation would escalate until he was shouting at her and she was crying. With the help of a counselor, he was able to understand that her accusations might be a way for her to cover up

her memory loss, and that arguing only upset both of them. Instead of arguing he learned to respond to her accusations by acknowledging she was upset about her money. "Is there anything I can do?" This calmed her down. (p. 3)

Beyond teaching families the importance of understanding the meaning of the patient's behavior and ways to respond appropriately, practitioners should encourage participation in a self-help group where, if nothing else occurs, family members learn ways of reducing the physical burdens of care. Self-help groups and counseling also help families to identify options for care and to explore the feasibility of placement in the least restrictive environment.

PRACTICE WITH THOSE BECOMING INSTITUTIONALIZED

Most important for professionals is to understand how aggression and magical mastery facilitate adaptation to long term care facilities. We have reported (Tobin & Lieberman, 1976) that before the actual entering and living in a facility, elderly people are transformed into what they have feared to become; that is, a person who can only survive by living in a nursing home. Concurrently, under the best of family circumstances, they feel abandoned by family, separated from them with little or no possibility of reunion. Giving in to their feelings can lead to hastened death, whereas handling these feelings by aggressiveness and magical coping can limit the adverse effects of stress.

Feelings of Family Members

What about the feelings of family members? Depressed and guilty, a decision to institutionalize an elderly family member is never taken lightly. By the time it occurs, the family often feels relieved but not without feeling of heightened inadequacy and, moreover with great rate. As discussed earlier the rage is toward oneself for being inadequate and rage toward the elderly person for inducing feelings of inadequacy. Too often, workers focus on the family's feelings of guilt, rather than on the accompanying feeling of inadequacy and rage, as well as sense of relief, after institutionalization. Given this mixture of painful feelings, it is expected that reassurances of competent care by personnel in facilities would be welcomed by families; and also welcomed would be subtle, and not so subtle, messages that it is not necessary to visit so much. It is indeed painful to visit a mother who is quickly deteriorating and may not recognize you. Visits by family members, however, are particularly important because of the effects of becoming institutionalized when old.

Attenuating Institutional Effects

When an elderly person is institutionalized in a long-term facility, the potentially deselfing process can be attenuated, in part, by interaction with family members. One common example is the importance of family visits to the seemingly intractably confused elderly resident of an institution. The elderly person may seem to be totally unaware of the family visitor at the time of the visit. Shortly after the visit, however, the elderly resident may become quite agitated, reflecting an awareness at some level of the visit; followed by a period in which organized reminiscence replaces psychotic like ramblings. Although important to the resident, the visit can be quite upsetting to the family visitor and serve only to heighten the previously discussed feelings of guilt, impotence and rage. Unless someone explains to the family the specific meaningfulness of the visit, the family may reduce their visiting, which can be quite harmful to the elderly resident. Chapter 5 contains a fuller discussion of preservation of the self during and after institutionalization in nursing homes.

WHO IS THE CLIENT?

Working with families challenges us to determine who is the client. Hopefully as noted earlier, we do not trade off the good of our elderly clients for the good of their caregivers. But it is never an easy task, especially when the emotional pain associated with caregiving to a deteriorating elderly family member is too much to bear:

Mr. Brown, an 80-year-old man had taken care of his wife, a victim of Alzheimer's disease, for six years. By the time she no longer recognized him, he was malnourished, overmedicated, and in congestive heart failure. When he was told by their long-time family physician that, "It's time" [time to send her to a nursing home], he wept uncontrollably. Childless, he knew he had no other choice. About one year later, when interviewed by a student, he was an active and visible participant in a senior center. He refused to talk about his wife who was in a vegetative state in the nursing home, but instead insisted on talking about the many activities in which he was engaged. He said that his only trouble was that he could not sleep, and as he talked about his insomnia, it became apparent that when alone at night he felt terribly guilty. Because he cannot bear to visit his wife, she lacks the preservation of self that might possibly be evoked by his face-to-face interaction with her. The last time he visited his wife, he wept uncontrollably for several days and even thought about suicide.

The worker of the senior center thought it would be helpful for this man to move from the house in which he has lived for over 40 years, where every stick of furniture reminds him of his institutionalized wife, to a residential setting where he could surround himself with memorabilia that provides him with more pleasant recollections. Until he makes his wishes known, this or any other solution would be projecture. But, apparently, Mr. Brown is unwilling to discuss this possibility and avoided beginning a therapeutic relationship.

Because it is too easy to identify with the burden on adult children who are closer in age to the therapist, it is imperative that the therapeutic alliance be primarily with the older person. Grunes (1987) has recommended that the first interview be only with the elder person and afterwards family members included. Berezin (1987), however, advocates beginning the therapeutic process by interviewing the older person and family members together because of the more comprehensive portrait of family dynamics that can be obtained. Yet, Coe (1987), after reviewing the literature on medical encounters between physicians and older people in which family members participated, concluded that collusion between physicians and family members is the norm and diminishes communication with, as well as a sensitivity to, the older patient. One reason for the collusion is the desire of the physician and other health professionals for the patient to comply with the therapeutic regimen. To be covered in the next chapter (Chapter 4), however, is the issue of compliance and passivity.

Reducing Psychological Distress from Hospitalizations

The causes for psychological distress that will be focused upon in this chapter are classified as iatrogenic. Iatrogenesis refers, in a narrow sense, to deleterious effects induced inadvertently by a physician in his or her treatment. The awareness that iatrogenic illness can result from treatment is reflected in the Hippocratic tradition in which physicians are directed to do no harm, at least to favor good in the balance of good over harm in treatment. Because physicians are not alone in inadvertently doing harm, a broadened definition is used here to encompass effects by health care personnel, in addition to physicians, and also by hospital policies and procedures.

The chapter begins with a brief introduction to the greater susceptibility of elderly patients to adverse effects from iatrogenic causes. Next is a section on expectations, particularly on how expectations of hospital personnel regarding Alzheimer's disease and depression become self-fulfilling prophecies for their elderly patients. A case is used to illustrate how the expectations of dementia cause hospital personnel to interpret depressed patients' inattention to their environments (a "pseudo" or false dementia) as Alzheimer's disease. To the extent that the depression is from self-blame and that accompanying passivity is from compliance, mobilizing aggressiveness, even combativeness, can be helpful to patients. The focus then shifts to issues of patients' "autonomy," the latest *linqua franca* for patients' self-determination. The importance of feelings of being in control, of mastery and successfully coping, are reaffirmed; and, specifically, the importance of promoting the kind of autonomy each patient needs to preserve an idiosyncratic self, one's idiosyncratic identity. The chapter ends with a brief comment on discharge planning.

SUSCEPTIBILITY OF THE ELDERLY

Patients of all ages are susceptible to hospital iatrogenesis but elderly patients are particularly susceptible because of less physiological homeostatic reserve and their multiplicity of illnesses. Also, the presence of many illnesses makes it common for elderly people to be treated with many medications when hospitalized. Whereas diverse specialists may prescribe appropriate medications for the conditions that they are treating, the accumulation and interaction of drugs can indeed cause adverse consequences. A geriatrician, from a medication review, can, however, usually reduce the number of drugs and also substitute interacting drugs with other noninteracting drugs and thereby reduce complications.

The significance of survival capacity among older persons was quite evident in our studies of relocation. The effects of stress among more healthy elderly persons was likely to be reflected in greater morbidity, physical illness, but among less healthy elderly persons it was likely to be reflected in mortality; that is, in a hastening of death. For example, among debilitated state hospital patients, a mortality rate of 18% was found within one year after relocation, as contrasted to only 6% among a control group that was not relocated.

Hospital iatrogenesis became of interest to me early in my career, during my clinical training at Drexel Home for the Aged. Residents of the home that were transferred temporarily to the hospital, even with careful following by the Home's Medical Director, were likely to be returned confused and depressed, and with needless medication to improve psychological status. Discussions at staff meetings often suggested that residents' confusion or depression was induced by hospital practices. It was not uncommon, for example, for the Medical Director to comment on how a drug given in too high a dose to one of our hospitalized elderly residents was likely to be responsible for his or her medical complication, a complication that included or led to confusion or depression, or sometimes both. Or the psychiatrist would comment that once again night hospital personnel misinterpreted cyclical sleep patterns and gave medication to induce sleep; but while it helped the patient to sleep, it also caused drowsiness and lethargy throughout the day. Then a member of the Nursing or Social Services Departments would tell about the resident who returned from the hospital quite depressed because of how floor personnel acted. Our hospitalized residents frequently reacted strongly to being chided for minor infractions of hospital rules, such as turning the TV set on too loud which was necessary because of impaired hearing. Calling the elegant Mrs. Weiss by her first name, which was taboo to do in the Home except by her closest friends, obviously worsened the situation.

A rare exception to considering this topic in geriatric medicine texts is the chapter, "Iatrogenesis," in *Essentials of Clinical Geriatrics* (2nd ed.) (Kane, Ouslander, & Brass, 1989). The chapter begins with a discussion of the narrowing of the therapeutic window with age as a consequence of the decreasing responsivity to therapy and the increasing susceptibility to toxic effects. Although they note that the "therapeutic window is perhaps more easily recognized in the pharmacological treatment of the elderly" (p. 332), they add such common iatrogenic problems as bed rest, enforced dependency, transfer trauma, and overzealous labeling of dementia and incontinence. Labeling is of particular relevancy for psychological effects and is a function of expectations of elderly patients that can indeed be harmful to them.

IATROGENIC PSYCHOLOGICAL EFFECTS

Despite the many possible causes for iatrogenic psychological effects, investigators have invariably attributed greater complication rates among elderly patients to their initial medical condition. For example, Steele et al. (Steele, 1984; Steele et al., 1981) reported that the increase in complications with age was largely a result of the number of drugs given for medical conditions at admission. Although he looked for psychiatric disturbances from other iatrogenic causes, his search was thwarted because there was inadequate documentation in medical records. In turn, Jahnigen et al. (1982), in commenting on psychiatric complications, noted that "nearly a fifth of the elderly on the medical service in our study experienced significant decompensation" (p. 390). Causes for decompensation were not specified, but others have speculated on causality: "environmental change and sensory alteration often go unrecognized" as causes of mental malfunctioning (Roslaniee & Fitzpatrick, 1979) and from prolonged mobilization (Miller, 1975). Obviously, there is an awareness among practitioners that there are many iatrogenic causes for confusion and depression in hospitalizations.

Confusion and Depression

The causes of confusion and depression, for convenience, can be divided into preadmission and postadmission causes; and, in turn, between physiological and psychosocial causes. Preadmission physiological causes include medical status, medications and nutritional status; and psychosocial causes include the lack of social supports and disruptive meanings of hospitalization. Postadmission physiological causes include diagnostic tests and procedures, treatments, medications, nutrition, sleep deprivation, immobilization; and psychosocial causes include social dislocation, encompassing depersonalization by staff, physical and emotional isolation and labelling. Social dislocation to a hospital, however, is more than living in a foreign environment. Beyond the geography and routines being different, the removing of personal belongings augments depersonalization (Goffman, 1961). Then, the wearing of a hospital gown like all other patients and residing in a sterile hospital room can only compound depersonalization. Furthermore, pre- and postadmission causes may interact when, for example, admission in poor medical status necessitates additional medications while in the hospital, or when a lack of social supports causes a greater pre-admission fear of nursing home placement leading to anxiety, agitation and sleep deprivation after admission.

Expectations of Alzheimer's Disease

The most obvious expectations that induce iatrogenesis are anticipations of Alzheimer's disease and depression. Illustrative is a case in which Alzheimer's disease was wrongly diagnosed:

In common with other elderly hospitalized patients, when my aunt Frieda was hospitalized in California, family members urged her to be a good patient. To Frieda being a good patient was not only to "do what the doctors order" but also not to bother any of the staff with requests or complaints. Initially she was only anxious but then she also became apathetic and withdrawn. The charge nurse noted this change and suggested to one of the house staff physicians, a first year resident in internal medicine, to call in a psychiatrist. When my cousin told me a psychiatric consultant had been requested, I immediately called the charge nurse who told me that my aunt was obviously confused and may have Alzheimer's disease. I responded that it was unlikely that she had Alzheimer's disease because three days before, when she was admitted to the hospital, she was oriented to time and place. I then suggested that my aunt had pseudodementia (a "false dementia" when depressed) because in her apathetic state she was unconcerned about where she was and the time of day or month. I also discussed my fear that a psychiatric resident unfamiliar with the causes for disorientation among elderly hospitalized patients would be too quick to suggest medication that could interact with her other medications. Since her brief admission to the hospital the number of drugs in her polypharmacy had risen at an alarming rate as she began to be seen by a variety of specialists for her diverse ailments. Also, a sedative would only increase her passivity. I then suggested waiting on the consultation until I could talk to my aunt.

My phone call to her revealed not only her apathy but also her anger which she was trying valiantly to hide in her determination to be a good patient. She was, however, enraged at her daughter, my cousin, for what she perceived as attempts to control her, at her physician for not being more definite in his diagnosis and treatment, and at the nurses for making her follow their routines. After I told her that she must speak up and not permit the anger to be bottled up within her, she began to reveal her suppressed anger. Deflecting her anger toward me, she bitterly said, "What do you expect me to do!" She felt impotent, unable to cope with her dreadful situation. I responded that it was her life and that if she wanted something, it was up to her to speak out. The conversation then abruptly ended when she said, in a voice that was barely audible, that she was too tired to talk.

The following afternoon my cousin called and vilified me for making her mother angry. No longer was mother a good patient! After my cousin's twenty minute tirade, I interjected a question on her mother's behavior. She was now getting out of bed and certainly more oriented in place and time. The conversation ended with my cousin acknowledging these improvements but still bitter regarding my interference.

In this instance, an elderly person was successfully mobilized. As frequently occurs, however, it is not always to the betterment of relations with others. My cousin still recalls how upsetting it was to her when her mother started to be an ornery patient. As discussed in the previous chapter, behaviors that are best for the elderly may indeed be discomforting to family members, but Frieda is also a classic illustration of how expectations lead to interpreting of behaviors as signs of dementia among elderly hospitalized patients. Her inability to locate herself in time and place was quick to be assessed as Alzheimer's disease when it was actually a result of her depression and thus a pseudodementia. Paradoxically, the charge nurse, who had revealed to me that she was trained in geriatric nursing, believed that she was not only acting correctly but acting more professionally than nurses untrained in geriatric nursing because she was aware that older patients may be suffering from Alzheimer's disease. Calling in a psychiatrist appeared to her to be the best of professional practice. Yet, if the psychiatrist was not sufficiently educated to Alzheimer's disease, and additionally chose to intervene vigorously by using potent psychotropic drugs, not only could the drugs lead to iatrogenic effects but so too could diagnostic procedures employed to rule out all other causes for a presumptive diagnosis of Alzheimer's disease.

"Sundowning"

Also, unfortunately, not too uncommon is to interpret the confusion in "sundowning" as Alzheimer's disease. Sundowning refers to the rather prevalent confusion in hospitalized patients as evening approaches. The combination of a foreign environment and drowsiness from bedfastness and soporific medication is likely to cause a transient confusion as daylight fades. Although sundowning occurs independent of age, it is more likely to be interpreted as Alzheimer's disease among elderly patients. Again, a quick history can reveal that the confusion is not part of the insidious progressive symptomatology characteristic of Alzheimer's disease. Rather, the patient is suffering from an acute episode that contradicts the diagnosis of Alzheimer's disease.

Reacting to a Foreign Environment

The foreignness of the environment per se can be a cause for confusion. As a member of a geriatric consultation team at a major teaching hospital, I became familiar with innumerable patients whose confusion was caused by the newness of environment.

Mrs. Andrews was found to be wandering in the hall at 2 a.m. and was unsure of where she was. She was extremely agitated but with a few reassuring words became calm. She did not want to return to her room but rather wanted to call her daughter to take her home immediately. With more assurance, she regained her composure, as well as orientation and returned to her bed.

In the morning, her daughter confided to the nurse that her mother had gotten up to urinate but because she did not know the location of the toilet, wet herself. An extremely fastidious woman, Mrs. Andrews then became extremely upset with consequent confusion and agitation.

Fortunately for Mrs. Andrews the night nurse recognized the acute quality of the confusion and did not overrespond. The recognition by her that nocturnal urination is common among the elderly and can, in turn, lead to wetting oneself in a foreign environment was evidenced in a later comment by the night nurse, "Mrs. A. reminds me of my mother. If she were to wet her panties like that, she would even be in worse shape. Whenever she gets anxious, she can't think or doesn't think right. She would think she had Alzheimers disease." These comments certainly capture the disorganizing force of a foreign environment, as well as the greater disorganization of behavior by anxiety among older persons than among younger persons.

An essential cause for Mrs. Andrews' anxiety was her feelings of loss of control. For her, fastidiousness is a way of mastering the world. Wetting herself made her feel that control was lost and not to be regained and, if the night nurse was correct, that she was not suffering from Alzheimer's disease. Fortunately, a perceptive nurse responded calmly and helped Mrs. Andrews to regain her sense of control. Had another nurse with a different response been on the floor, Mrs. Andrews' confusion and agitation may have persisted and led to needless medication with possibly further iatrogenic effects.

Depression

Frieda illustrates the role of depression in fulfilling the expectation that elderly patients who are confused are suffering from dementia. Yet, because Frieda's depression was not expressed in a dramatic form, but rather in apathy and suppressed anger, hospital personnel did not respond to the depression. They are, however, likely to have the erroneous belief that the elderly suffer more from clinical depression than persons of other ages. But epidemiological studies have clearly revealed that the elderly have no greater incidence of clinical depression (Blazer et al., 1987; Gurland et al., 1980). As with the expection of Alzheimer's disease, expectations of depression can lead to treatment that can cause iatrogenic effects. To expect that elderly patients will be clinically depressed because of a multiplicity of losses can cause a disregard for obvious reasons for depressions that may be handled without the kinds of interventions that can cause iatrogenic effects.

For example, a rather frequent phenomenon in hospitals that causes over-medication is when the elderly patient is told that "It's time to enter a nursing home." Typical is the case of the elderly woman patient who was given medication for her depression and when the depression lifted, attributing success to the drug:

When Mrs. Carson a widowed lady of eighty two with no family had been told shortly after being admitted to the hospital that it was not possible for her to return home, she became depressed for which she was medicated. Unresponsive to queries used to assess her mental status, an immediate diagnosis of dementia was made. Fortunately, however, a geriatric nurse surmised that the deterioration was really a pseudodementia, and not a true dementia, because shortly before she became depressed she was perfectly lucid. The nurse, moreover appreciated the cause for Mrs. Carson's depression which resulted from the realization that she would not return home. Yet, the geriatric nurse felt that it was necessary to medicate Mrs. Carson and communicated her feelings to the attending physician.

As Mrs. Carson wrestled with her problem that she had no alternative but to enter a long-term care facility, she began to consider the necessity of a nursing home that would sustain her, that would help her survive. Eventually she decided that the County home, to which a friend had gone, would be suitable for her. With this resolution the depression lifted.

As accomplished by elderly people who adapt best to institutionalization, Mrs. Carson transformed the situation so that the decision to enter a nursing home became her own and, also, the nursing home she chose became an ideal environment for her. She then began to talk about the gains that would accrue from entering the County nursing home. She would make friends and participate in activities. The loss of independence in relinquishing her apartment receded into the background and she appropriately focused on the impending event.

There was no need to medicate Mrs. Carson. Her medication did not alleviate the depression but, rather, her working through the decision that "It's time . . ." was the cause for its alleviation. What could have helped Mrs. Carson was assistance in transforming the dreaded reality of nursing home placement into an acceptable solution through the use of magical coping. Without this assistance, Mrs. Carson was able to transform the situation to her liking but she may be one of the few patients able to do so. Others are less fortunate in being unable to transform the situation without professional assistance.

Other Expectations

Another kind of harmful expectation relates to accepting verbalizations reflecting accommodations to impairments as the absence of impairments. If, for example, very old patients are asked if they have sensory problems, hearing, visual losses, or back pains, they are likely to report "no problems." But accommodations to impairments does not mean that problems are not present nor that these problems cannot be treated. Ninety year olds are less likely than eighty year olds to complain of problems and eighty year olds less likely than seventy year olds. If mobile and lucid, and the self is preserved, as discussed in Chapter 1, complaints are likely to be fewer. Yet accommodation to treatable deficits must be understood and whenever possible, deficits remediated. These sins of omission can also be considered as a kind of iatrogenesis.

A more flagrant kind of iatrogenesis is evident when it is expected that a percentage of elderly patients will suffer from a condition associated with disease. For example, among debilitated bedridden patients, pressure sores will occur. To accept any percentage as unavoidable, however, is to dismiss the possibility of preventing pressure sores that may be preventable.

Iatrogenic effects, in combination with the conditions warranting hospital admission, can quicken the transition from being "older" and "elderly" to being "old," and produce expectations among hospital personnel that older people in general have become "old."

A new social worker remarked that people in their seventies are usually depressed. She illustrated her comments with a visibly depressed woman who had been admitted for COPD (Chronic Obstructive Pulmonary Disease). Mrs. Burke, the worker said, was preoccupied with whether she would be bedridden and would have to go to a nursing home. Although weepy and only able to communicate in a strained sad voice, Mrs. Burke would frequently say, "It's come. I can't care for myself. I'm too old." The worker did not recognize that it was her fears of being immobile and possible nursing home placement that evoked the current feelings of becoming old and not her chronological age. Yet, if Mrs. Burke recovered sufficiently to care for herself at home, a possibly premature transition to becoming "old" may have been reversed. Because she was not followed through after discharge, her disposition and later affect status is unknown.

Mrs. Burke, like others, when under the duress of hospitalization, can undergo the transition to becoming "old" and often, besides being preoccupied with immobility and nursing home placement, become preoccupied with how death will occur, an issue that will be discussed in Chapter 7 on accepting death. And, like others, when hospitalized patients become melancholic, they are likely to be unable to use the beneficial psychological mechanisms of aggressiveness and blending the present and the past, as well as making the past vivid, to reaffirm the sense of a persistent identity.

AUTONOMY OF PATIENTS

Patient self-determination, as noted earlier, is now usually discussed as "autonomy" which, by definition, refers to self-rule encompassing familiar attributes such as liberty, independence and freedom of choice. From a psychological perspective, the feeling of autonomy is akin to a sense of control, of feeling in control rather than feeling controlled by others. Within the general attention to the autonomy of elderly people, most attention has been focused on the importance for impaired elderly patients to participate in decision-making in affairs that concern them. Witness the 1988 supplementary issue of *The Gerontologist* entitled "Autonomy and Long Term Care," in which an assumption of authors of articles is that the exclusion of participation in decisions reduces self-determination and thereby, a sense of control over one's life. From this perspective, autonomy has both an objective and subjective aspect where the objective aspect refers to enhancement of self-determination through removal of manifest barriers and the subjective aspect refers to the latent, more personal experience of self-determination, of being in control over one's life.

When autonomy is the focus in the care of patients, it is most often on objective autonomy in nursing homes. It is on the presence of barriers to self-determination such as the freedom to choose what to wear, when to arise in the morning or what types of food to eat, and so forth. To be sure, whereas the removal of these, and all barriers, must not be minimized, practice must go further. A personal, idiosyncratic sense of autonomy within each patient must be enhanced. An enhancement of a subjective personal sense of autonomy is, however, a great deal more difficult than removing objective barriers to autonomy.

Indeed, an enhancement of a subjective personal sense of autonomy, a sense of control, for some patients may, paradoxically entail assisting them to maintain life-long dependent nonautonomous relationships with others. The somewhat paranoid patient (more frequently, the resident in a nursing home), whose paranoia is functional, may best be able to preserve his or her unique sense of self or identity, if paired with a "paranee," a roommate whose sense of self necessitates accepting blame by others.

Why Focus on Autonomy?

The primary reason for focusing on autonomy is simple: Current practices and policies diminish the autonomy of chronically ill patients. In turn, it has been the practices and policies of nursing homes that has been the almost exclusive focus of attention in writings on how autonomy is diminished among chronically ill older patients. Here, however, in a novel effort, the focus will be on autonomy-related issues for their relevancy for understanding iatrogenesis in acute hospital settings.

Three kinds of justifications have been proffered by Hofland (1988) for focusing on autonomy. First is the justification emanating from the law mandating that everyone is to be given due process and equal protection which may not be so for elderly with chronic impairments. Second is the justification intrinsic to medical ethics necessitating health professionals to use their expertise to seek the greater balance of good over harm which, unfortunately, can lead to paternalism and thus incursions on autonomy. A third justification, specific to chronic care, is the challenge to modify policies and practice when there is no cure; when, that is, patients have knowledge regarding their adaption to diseases and disabilities that transcends the expert knowledge of health professionals.

Autonomy and the Law. The fundamental laws that govern the rights of individuals in our society guarantees to all citizens due process and equal protection. Yet, as noted by Hofland (1988), the "rights of frail and impaired older people are often abridged in the policies and admission procedures of nursing homes and compromised in discharge-planning and guardianship procedures" (p. 4). Because the kinds of care required by increasing numbers of frail elderly may tend to limit their fundamental freedoms, Thomasma (1985) has conjectured that the "next great civil rights issue in the United States may well be that of persons in long-term care" (p. 225).

Autonomy and Medical Ethics. One reason why the provision of required care can inevitably lead to limitations of fundamental freedoms relates to our medical ethics. The Hippocratic tradition delineates the moral responsibility of beneficence (Beauchamp & McCullough, 1984) which directs physicians to promote and protect the best interests of patients by seeking the greater balance of good over harm in treatment and care. Because physicians define patients' best interests, medical care is by its very nature paternalistic (Childress, 1982; Veatch, 1981). High technology therapeutics have augmented paternalism by providing physicians with ways of increasing the good. In turn, decreasing the bad, so that again the balance of good over bad is maximized, leads to paternalism by making decision for debilitated patients that would otherwise lead to untoward consequences if patients made their own decisions. The raising of bed rails so that the very old hospitalized patient with brittle bones will not sustain a fracture when arising at night to urinate is an example of paternalism to reduce harm. Clearly, patients' personal autonomy is not an intrinsic value in this decision nor is it in other aspects of medical care. Yet can we argue that whereas personal autonomy may not be intrinsic to acute care, personal autonomy is indeed intrinsic to chronic care?

Autonomy in Chronic Care. It has been asserted that in acute care the physician-patient relationships must be paternalistic because it is inherently characterized by inequities of knowledge (see Komrad, 1983). Chronic care, however, may be different because the balance of knowledge may be different. When cure is not possible, the relationship between physicians and patients is decidedly different with a greater degree of knowledge residing in patients regarding adaptation to their diseases and disabilities. Indeed, it is the tipping of this balance that causes many physicians to avoid practicing with those who have chronic diseases. Still, we can not abrogate our responsibility to provide professional care. And professional care demands that judgments are made regarding what is best for patients. The challenge is to temper the application of necessary professional judgments by a sensitivity to their iatrogenic sequela; that is, to the inadvertent adverse consequences of treatment, practices and policies.

ISSUES IN PATIENTS' AUTONOMY

Callopy (1988) in his conceptual framework for the supplementary issue of *The Gerontologist* identified six polarities that contain professional judgments that can limit personal autonomy. Each is instructive for understanding how the sense of control can be augmented or diminished.

Decisional versus Executional Autonomy

This polarity refers to the ability and freedom to make decisions versus the ability to carry them out. Although it is optimum to have both kinds of autonomy, many patients do not have the capacity to act on their decisions. For these patients, that lack executional autonomy, if there is too narrow a focus on what can be executed, there are likely to be restrictions on permitting any decisions and, surely, a diminution of any sense of control. The elderly man recovering from a hip replacement may not yet be able to ambulate but if lucid, should be allowed to make as many decisions for himself as possible. Indeed, he should be encouraged to make decisions for himself because to be immobile is to feel particularly vulnerable, impotent and useless. It is often immobility that causes older persons to make the transition to now being "old." This transition can sometimes be avoided by encouraging decisions and then providing assistance in carrying them out even if their execution is difficult or nearly impossible. The elderly woman who has remained for weeks or months in the acute hospital while awaiting a nursing home bed (e.g., the hospitalized patient in an ALC [alternative level of care] bed), who cannot dress herself because of crippling arthritis, must not only be encouraged to select what clothes to wear everyday but also assisted in dressing even if difficult, tedious and time consuming for workers on the unit.

Direct versus Designated Autonomy

This polarity refers to deciding or acting on one's own versus giving authority to others to decide or to act. Necessary often is a blend of both but with explicit, mutually accepted responsibilities. The negotiating process that occurs when an elderly parent moves into an adult son's or daughter's home, for example, should contain an admixture of direct and designated autonomy. More complicated is when a patient assigns durable power of attorney to a family member. In this instance, it is expected that the family member will make the appropriate decision whether or not to terminate life if unable to do for oneself as when comatose. This autonomy that is designated to a family member extends to the physician who is requested to act on the patient's and family's behalf (e.g., to write orders to remove a nasogastric tube or write DNR [do not resuscitate] orders).

Competent versus Incompetent Autonomy

The third polarity recognizes the incompetence of many mentally impaired elderly persons to make rational decisions. Yet global and perfunctory judgments of incompetence must be avoided. Indeed, the reasoning of those whose logical choices seem so unreasonable to us must be respected:

The elderly cardiac patient who refused treatment for his prostate cancer because he reasoned that he is likely to die from heart failure before painful uremic poisoning, struck us as irrational. But the Geriatric Consultation Team had to seriously consider the wishes of this formerly physically active retired truck driver who said, "I don't want anybody to touch me down there." Concurrently his daughter said, "He has always been sort of kooky about his manhood. So we shouldn't listen to what he says and do everything we can do to help dad." His daughter could not easily be dissuaded to abide by her father's wishes and her father persisted in not wanting the operation. A cardiac specialist, in his late seventies, was called in who concluded that it was equally likely that he would die from uremic poisoning as from cardiac complications but, also, adamantly defended the patient's right to make his own decision. Only after much cajoling did the daughter relent to her father's decision.

To be sure, there is no simple answer to what is professional responsibility in this instance, as well as in many other instances.

Authentic versus Inauthentic Autonomy

This polarity makes a distinction between choices and action that are consistent versus inconsistent with character. Only through attention to idiosyncratic characteristics of individuals is it possible to enhance Authentic Autonomy. Too little attention, unfortunately, is given to understanding who patients are and how to assist them in being themselves, an omission which occurs even when there is the best of intentions.

Mrs. O'Brien, a 75-year-old dehydrated and malnourished woman, was transferred to the general hospital from a psychiatric hospital following an attempt to starve herself to death. The discussion at the multidisciplinary geriatric staff conference focused on the rights of patients to terminate their lives if they no longer wished to live. There was a consensus that Mrs. O'Brien was undergoing an "existential crisis" and how felt hopeless and forlorn but was not clinically depressed. The kind of hopelessness perceived to be evidenced by Mrs. O'Brien is apparently associated with suicide. Although the tone of the discussion suggested agreement that she had a right to do away with her life, counseling was recommended to reestablish a reason for living. Because she had been a writer of children's books, one approach suggested was to encourage her to write; to compose, for example, her autobiography.

When Mrs. O'Brien was brought into the conference to be interviewed, it was my impression that her stated wish to commit suicide did not ring true. To be sure, a few weeks earlier she began to starve herself and had not a neighbor come by to say hello, she would have been successful. Yet something had changed and now it appeared that she was not suicidal. What had changed was that a male attendant befriended her and reestablished for her a lifelong pattern of being admired by men for her cleverness and wit. Her comments on her past revealed that her intellectual father had admired his precocious daughter, his only child, and also that her husband was so in love with her that he agreed that having children would only detract from their love. It was rather evident that she did not want a child to compete for her husband's love and that without children, she could reenact being the only and special child with her husband. After her husband's death she was able to maintain this interpersonal dynamic by taking a young artist into her house. When he left, the crises began that led to her decision to do away with herself.

Unfortunately, Mrs. O'Brien would soon be discharged from the hospital without the male aide. Counseling her to return to writing did not appear necessary. Unless admired by a man, her writing apparently by itself had little meaning. For her, feeling admired by a man was a pre-condition for the gratification she obtained from writing childrens literature, apparently playing out the little girl in herself. Necessary was placement in a non-institutional setting in which she could maintain her lifelong sense of self. A social worker was able to identify an adult home that had a male administrator who was certain to be enchanted by Mrs. O'Brien.

Only through an understanding of Mrs. O'Brien's persistent way of relating to others, and also the psychodynamics reflected in these relationships, was it possible to appreciate the shift from her wished for death to her wish for life. Whereas I believe, as many do, that we should allow self-determination in deciding to end one's life, we must be cautious in interpreting patients' wishes. For the patient who requests DNR (do not resuscitate), the decision to let the patient die, passive euthanasia, may sometimes be made rather easily. But for Mrs. O'Brien and for other patients who are fully lucid, it is our challenge to attempt to reestablish authentic autonomy, a preservation of the self, although the patient may resist our efforts to do so.

Immediate versus Long-Range Autonomy

This polarity recognizes the tensions inherent in providing freedom here-and-now that may limit long-range autonomy and, conversely, limiting freedom now so that there will be greater long-range autonomy. Daytime wanderers' lounges for confused institutionalized patients have been found to enhance cognitive organization and also to be associated with less of a need for medication and better sleeping habits when returned to their unit (McGrowder-Linn & Bhatt, 1988). Yet, some patients must initially be forced to go to the lounge and to leave the protection of their unit. Forcefully encouraging elderly patient to walk after surgery is only one of the examples that are too numerous to mention when even efforts that often times look like coercion are warranted so that long-range gains can be made. Infringement on immediate autonomy can indeed enhance long range personal autonomy, especially for confused patients because unless, that is, intractable confusion is ameliorated, there can be no rational decision-making on one's own behalf. Indeed, a modicum of lucidity is a necessary precursor for rational and purposive decision-making.

Negative versus Positive Autonomy

In the sixth, and final, of Callopy's polarities, negative autonomy refers to removing barriers that limit autonomy, whereas positive autonomy refers to promoting autonomy. An extreme case of inattention to positive autonomy, to promoting personhood occurred in April 1989:

Miss Coons, 86, was comatose in the hospital for five months. Because of the persistence of her coma, her sister, age 83, implored her sister's physician and lawyer to remove her gastric feeding tube and finally to let her sister die a natural death. A judge agreed. Nursing staff, however, feared that other patients would perceive them as letting them die too. Reassurances however, only heightened the anxiety of these patients and the nurses became even more resistant to removing the gastric tube. When the tube was removed, not only did the nurses begin to feed Ms. Coons and to care for her, but also the other patients became very attentive to Ms. Coons. Apparently, the attention, the skin contact she lacked for five months, helped to revive her as she slowly came out of her coma.

The next day at a meeting, one of the most prestigious geriatricians in the community told me that this was not the first time that there was a beneficial effect for an elderly comatose patient who was assumed beyond help. He added that it was not all that rare among patients he had treated over several decades. We agreed that unless there are active, and sometimes vigorous, attempts to humanize care and to reestablish a sense of personhood, it should not be assumed that an irreversible state with no quality to life is present.

DISCHARGE PLANNING

The cases presented in this chapter include references to discharge dispositions. Indeed, curative treatment in hospitals is inseparable from discharge planning which must begin as soon as possible. Without considerations of after hospital placement and care, treatment can be misguided:

I was asked by the Chief of the in-patient psychiatry unit to consult on a depressed patient in his late seventies who had suffered a psychotic depressive episode 30 years before when he was in his forties which had been resolved with electric shock therapy. Although I was unaware of my task when I accepted the assignment, I was expected to convince Mr. Lawrence to again accept shock treatments. On the day I was to consult on Mr. Lawrence I was told that he had become even more depressed and now was mute.

After the psychiatric resident presented Mr. Lawrence's history, a marginal person who had minimal attachments to others, we briefly discussed the precipitating events that had led to his current hospitalization on a locked psychiatric unit. Mr. Lawrence had been living alone and because of the inclement weather had not shopped for food and had become increasingly malnourished and dehydrated. A neighbor called the police when she realized she had not seen Mr. Lawrence recently and feared that he had died in his apartment. On entering his apartment, it was apparent that Mr. Lawrence was incoherent. She called the police who took him to the emergency room, where a short conversation between Mr. Lawrence and the psychiatric resident on call led to a psychiatric rather than to an acute medical unit.

When Mr. Lawrence was wheeled into the conference room, I noted that despite a face that was fixed in a depressive demeanor, he raised his eyes slightly to look around the room and for a moment fixed on two young female psychiatric residents who were attending the staff conference. He was wheeled about two feet away from me and I pulled up my chair, gently touched him on his wrist and said something to the effect "It's nice being the center of attention of attractive young ladies." Although it seemed like five minutes, he slowly opened his eyes and slightly turned his head to look at me. We then began our conversation. He was aware that he had not been eating properly and that each day he had told himself he must go out to buy food. He apparently blacked out and awoke very frightened in a cold sweat and disoriented. He was reluctant to discuss the depressive episode 30 years ago, but it was apparent that he feared that once again he would receive shock treatments.

Rather abruptly, his psychiatrist asked if he could talk to the patient and he too pulled up a chair very close to Mr. Lawrence and asked "Would you be willing to sign the consent form so that we can give you shock treatment?" Immediately Mr. Lawrence's face returned to a taut depressed expression and he became mute, refusing to continue the conversation. Further questioning did not elicit any answers. After Mr. Lawrence was wheeled out of the room, the Chief of Service asked me how we could convince Mr. Lawrence to accept shock treatment. His psychiatrist, however, asked whether I thought shock was necessary. I sidestepped this question because the Chief of Service was determined to do so and I responded that I was more concerned with what will happen to Mr. Lawrence after his discharge. A lively discussion then ensued with the social worker who had been thinking about placement. It appeared both to her, and to me too, that discharge to an adult home where he would feel secure would be sensible, if not ideal, for Mr. Lawrence. All he wished at this time in his life was to be warm in winter and not to be hungry. Even a minimal amount of attention to those basic needs would indeed elicit a very favorable response from Mr. Lawrence.

A focus on discharge placement, rather than on his acceptance of electric shock therapy, would, I believe, have enormously benefited Mr. Lawrence. Attempts to communicate with him about his aftercare would, that is, probably have elicited some verbal comments, lifting his mutism; and talking to him about placement could have obviated the necessity for shock treatments, a procedure with obvious iatrogenic consequences for Mr. Lawrence who shudders when he recalls his shock treatments decades earlier.

Nowadays with patients being discharged "quicker and sicker," there is, however, too little opportunity to work through placement in a facility. The harassed discharge planner must, for example, tell families that they have almost no time at all to locate a nursing home. As they scramble to find an empty bed, under enormous strain if the elderly patient is on Medicaid (a "non-self-payer") or unable to feed him or herself ("a feeder"), workers are unable to adequately assist residents-to-be for the impending relocations. When, with great relief, a nursing home is found that they can justify as appropriate, relocation occurs swiftly and with increasing frequency, with no warning to the patient.

FINAL COMMENT

Iatrogenic psychological effects are nurtured daily in the hospital. In the *New York Times* on March 23, 1986, there was a review of Geisel's new book, *You're Only Old Once*. Commenting on his new Dr. Seuss book for adults he said, "I still climb Mount Everest just as often as I used to. I play polo just as often as I used to. But to walk down to the hardware store I found a little more difficult. I have a feeling if I stay out of hospitals I may live forever" (p. 13). Dr. Seuss then revealed how hospital personnel can indeed be harmful. When being wheeled into the operating room on a gurney for an eye operation, the attendant pulled out one of Dr. Seuss' books and asked him to autograph it. Dr. Seuss commented: "He probably thought it would be the last one I ever gave. It was very flattering but I wanted to sock him" (p. 13).

Given the risks to elderly patients in hospitals, special geriatric hospital units are being developed. Multidisciplinary geriatric assessment units are particularly invaluable because treatable conditions can be uncovered, rehabilitation begun and a plan of care developed to enable remaining in the community. Perhaps through these kinds of innovations the ratio of benefit to risk can be increased among hospitalized elderly patients reducing such common causes of hospital iatrogenesis as misguided expectations of labeling, excessive bed rest, as inattention to recuperation by carrying out activities of daily living, and insensitivities to the necessity to enhance authentic autonomy, to assure a sense of control and to preserve identities.

Chapter **5**

Providing Supportive Services in Nursing Homes

The main message of this chapter on supportive services in nursing homes is the necessity for structuring ongoing relationships between staff and individual residents. Indeed, the usefulness of sophisticated practitioners in nursing homes is less in their one-to-one interaction with residents than with their structuring of relationships. After discussion of some of these basic principles, knowledge about nursing home adaptation will be related to the necessity to enhance a sense of control throughout the process of becoming a resident of a nursing home. Then, in the next major section, the focus is on working with staff to develop psychosocial environments of high quality. Next is a discussion on behavioral interventions where the emphasis is on developing prosthetic environments (milieus that reinforce functional behaviors). The final section contains a report of an innovative approach to increasing the involvement of families with their institutionalized impaired members. Briefly, a structural approach to the deployment of staff was developed in which families were encouraged to relate one way to unit workers and in another way to administrative staff. Unit workers were neither social workers or nurses but, rather, individuals with bachelor degrees who could work comfortably with others. Using these unit workers permitted a relationship with the institution was nurtured (an "institutional transference") that was divided (a "split transference") between unit workers who were encouraged to be perceived as all-giving extensions of family and administrative staff who were encouraged to allow anger to be displaced onto them.

SOME BASIC PRINCIPLES

Some of the basic principles of working in nursing homes have been provided by Edelson and Lyons (1985) in the introduction to their excellent book *Institutional Care of the Mentally Impaired Elderly*. They begin by admonishing the reader not to confuse mental disease with treatable "excess disability." Expectations, for example, as discussed in the previous chapter, can too easily cause staff to discourage use of residual capacities of residents of their facilities who have organic brain damage. The authors note, as I did in Chapter 2, that Brody, Kleban, and their associates (Brody et al., 1971; Kleban et al., 1971) found that identifiable excess disabilities could be reduced or eliminated in an institutional setting among the more aggressive residents. Behaving aggressively, however, is likely to conflict with institutional views of effective management.

Edelson and Lyons then continue by stating that care must be provided "that is rehabilitative whenever possible, prosthetic whenever necessary, and at all times humane, identity-preserving, and ego-supporting" (p. xix). Identity-preserving is the same as preservation of the self and, of interest, is that in their next chapter, Edelson and Lyons explain how promoting mastery is the essence of ego-supporting efforts (using Goldfarb's formulation of inflating beliefs in mastery, which was discussed in Chapter 2 when focusing upon working with individuals).

Next Edelson and Lyons, from their many years of experience at the Baycrest Geriatric Center in Toronto, note that "institutional arrangements that support direct care staff in establishing a supportive relationship with impaired residents focuses attention on how interdisciplinary teams work" (p. xxi). Thus, individual mental health practitioners, separately or as members of teams, can best be used to structure ongoing supportive relationships between staff and individual residents.

Finally, they state: "As changes are made to meet the needs of the mentally impaired elderly, there will be resistance to change" (p. xxii). The obvious challenge to professionals is to facilitate change, but a paradox is that facilities must be assisted in changing so that they become settings where identities are not changed. Fortunately, mental health professionals are precisely those professionals who know only too well how hard it is to reduce resistance to change but, also, at the same time, know how to reduce the resistance.

BEFORE AND SOON AFTER ADMISSION

The creation of nursing home environments that preserve the self should follow from an understanding of inner experiences throughout the process of institutionalization and, also, of individual attributes and environmental characteristics predictive of adaptation. Our findings on process and predictors will form the basis for discussion of enhancing control throughout the process of becoming institutionalized when old.

A Synopsis of Findings

First to be discussed are findings on the process of becoming institutionalized including the preadmission redefinition of self, the postadmission first-month syndrome, and then the reestablishment of self. Next findings on the prediction of vulnerability to institutionalization will be covered.

Redefinition of Self Before Admission. As noted in previous chapters, the message that "It's time to go to a nursing home" evokes a painful and distressing change in self-concept. The resident-to-be has become what has been feared. That is, before placement is considered, the best nursing homes are perceived as assuring survival when no other alternatives are available. The underlying feeling, however, is that going to a nursing home is to be abandoned to a "death house" (Kuypers, 1969). Then when "It's time," the metamorphosis occurs to becoming the kind of person that has been dreaded.

Residents-to-be who successfully deal with the inner experience of being abandoned while awaiting admission to nursing homes focus on anticipations of physical care, security and activities (Pincus, 1968) and, as noted in Chapter 1, use magical coping, transforming the nursing home into an environment that is closer to the ideal and convincing oneself that the relocation is of their own choosing.

First-Month Syndrome. Entering and living in a foreign environment is associated with what Grunes (1959, personal communication) has labelled "the first month syndrome." Unless psychotic, the newly admitted resident will manifest behavioral changes. Some become quite disorganized, others become extremely depressed, and still others become both disorganized and depressed.

Reestablishment of Self. After the first month syndrome, most residents of nursing homes of good psychosocial quality are able to reestablish their self-pictures. Indeed, our data suggested great stability in the self-picture from before to two months after admission (see Tobin & Lieberman, 1976, *Last Home for the Aged*). The psychological portrait of residents by two months after admission approximated the portrait before admission. Adverse changes were limited to more hopelessness (less optimism about the future but not more clinical depression nor less life satisfaction); an increase in bodily preoccupation and a perception of less capacity for self care, suggesting the adoption of the role of patient among other old sick people; and a lessening of feelings of affiliation with others reflecting, apparently, an experience not unlike sibling rivalry with other residents.

Concurrently, there was an amelioration of the feelings of being abandoned by family (see also Smith & Bengtson, 1979). Indeed, the tendency was toward mythicizing of living children, reflected specifically in reminiscent data, which apparently is an exaggerated expression of the age-associated process of mythicizing significant figures from the past. Although a child may still be alive and a frequent visitor, the increased psychological distance created by institutionalization and the need to preserve the self in the face of institutional demands may cause an exaggeration in the mythicizing of this adult child. The exaggerated response is likely to be reinforced by the institutional environment where the coin of the realm is famous offsprings who are attentive and caring, and where family attention provides leverages for personal prestige and, also, for more attentive staff caring.

Although entering and living in the best of nursing homes was not associated with changes that would support belief in the "destructiveness of institutions," the shift at the more latent less conscious level was not, however, as modest as the manifest changes in psychological status. The earliest memories revealed a significant shift from abandonment toward the introduction of themes of mutilation and death. This shift in recollections sometimes occurred when the same incident was reported at both times:

Before admission Mrs. Wagner offered the following earliest memory: "I remember my mother. She had hair like braids, open and falling upon her shoulder. She was sitting up in her bed and near her on her table was a bottle of honey and I remember asking her for honey. That's all I remember—nothing before and nothing behind. I still can see her sitting in bed. I must have been two years, two or three. Closer to two, I guess. But that's a picture I have." After admission she recalled: "I remember my mother's death. I remember at least one moment of it. She had honey on her bed and I wanted some of that honey. I didn't really understand that she was dying. I was almost 3 years old. That's all I remember. I can see her face clearly even now. She had two braids hanging down. This picture is all I remember of her.

The contrast between the two memories suggests that a breakthrough of repression had occurred in which previously withheld, archaic material was now being expressed. It would appear that in the first report that pain of mother's death is defended against, but breaks through in the second telling of the same incident. In the reconstruction of the same incident at both times, there is a central theme of oral deprivation (e.g., wanting, but not getting, the honey), as well as the personally meaningful symbolism of mother's braids.

More often, however, the increase in loss when becoming institutionalized was associated with a shift in incidents, as in the following example of the repeat earliest memory.

When on the waiting list, Mrs. Rosen said, "I liked to go swimming and mother wouldn't let me. Once I stood on the pier and fell in. I remember how they took me out and took me to my mother. That's all I remember. I wasn't sick." And after admission: "Didn't have coffins in the old country like they do here. My father died. I remember my sister was still a breast baby. . . . It was a cold day. My mother said don't go. But he was a stubborn man and so he got pneumonia and died."

Contrasts with thematic changes in the control groups suggest that one-third would not have shifted to these themes of more narcissistic loss had they not entered the homes. The shift is, apparently, specifically related to entering and living in the homes, and to living in a total institutional environment with sick elderly in a home that is to be the last one. With such a significant shift, from abandonment to increased vulnerability, it was indeed surprising that so little change was observed in psychological status. Most likely the ability to successfully contain, to defend against, the latent meanings is a function of entering the best of contemporary long-term care facilities. Yet even these facilities exact their toll, as reflected in the latent meaning of institutional life itself, in the adoption of the patient role, in a lessening of futurity, and in portraying oneself as less willing to be close to others.

At the End of One Year

By the end of one year postadmission, more than one-half of the sample had either died or had extremely deteriorated. Those able to be interviewed again showed only a lessening of affiliation in relation to others and a lessening of body preoccupation. All other measures did not show a change. This pattern of stability with only focal changes in affiliation and body preoccupation among the intact survivors masks the global outcomes: 41 of our 85 institutionalized elderly people had died or had become extremely deteriorated. To what extent these forty one would have shown these outcomes had they not entered and lived in the nursing homes is impossible to know.

Predicting Vulnerability to the Stress of Institutionalization

Assessments of the possible psychological predictors of morbidity and mortality were made while on waiting lists preceding admission. Measures were sorted out into nine dimensions that have either been explicitly discussed as, or inferred to be, predictors of outcome to stress; functional capacities, affects, hope, the self-system, personality traits, reminiscence, coping with the impending event, interpersonal relations and accumulated stress. The two outcome groups (the intact survivors and the nonintact) were then contrasted on these measures, and simultaneously, the corresponding two outcome groups were contrasted for the two control samples. Thus, any measure that differentiated, or predicted, for the sample that underwent the stress of institutionalization and also predicted for the sample not undergoing this stress could not be a predictor of vulnerability to the stress of institutionalization but, rather, would be a characteristic associated with survival. Stated another way, if a measure only predicted for the sample undergoing stress could the attribute being measured be considered a sensitizer to the stress of institutionalization and not associated with survival per se.

Passivity. Measures in several dimensions were associated with survival (function capacities, affects, hope, self-system, coping, and interpersonal relations), but only one dimension was a sensitizer to the stress of institutionalization: Passivity was associated with morbidity and mortality among those entering the homes but not with morbidity and mortality for those in stable environments (also see Turner, Tobin, & Lieberman, 1972).

Magical Coping. A dimension that was not relevant for control samples was coping with the impending event of institutionalization. When residents on the waiting list were assessed, however, for how they were mastering the impending event of institutionalization, it was found that those who transformed the situation so as to make the move totally voluntary and also to perceive the relocation environment as ideal were those most likely to survive intact through one year following admission. As discussed in Chapter 1, this kind of magical coping (as well as aggressiveness and hopefulness) was found to enhance adaptation in three additional relocation situations which are described in the Lieberman and Tobin 1983 book *The Experience of Old Age.*

Environmental Quality. Not unexpectedly, the quality of the psychosocial environment also predicted outcomes. This was most clear in our fourth study, the en masse relocation of 427 state mental hospital patients to 142 nursing and boarding homes. The relocated group of 427 had a death rate one year after relocation of 18%, and the carefully matched control group of 100 who were not relocated had a death rate in the same interval of only 6%. Those who remained alive following the relocation were likely to have entered facilities of good psychosocial quality.

To be specific, the beneficial psychosocial qualities were, first, warmth expressed in interpersonal relations between residents and staff and, also, between residents; second, activities and other forms of stimulation that are perceived and interacted with; third, tolerance for deviancies such as aggression, drinking, wandering, complaining, and incontinence; and fourth, and lastly, individuation defined as the extent to which residents are perceived and treated as individuals in being allowed and encouraged to express individuality. It is a pattern of qualities that reflect the acceptance of aggressiveness, magical coping, myth-making in reminiscence, and, certainly, the preservation of self.

Control in Nursing Home Adaptation

Among the personal characteristics fostered by the survival-enhancing environments is a sense of control, a construct that has been introduced throughout this volume, for example, in the previous chapter when discussing autonomy and self-determination. The most impressive studies of control in nursing home adaptation have been carried out by Langer and Rodin (Langer & Rodin, 1976; Rodin & Langer, 1977). Langer, in her 1989 book *Mindfulness*, provides a full summary of their experiment on introducing control to nursing home residents. Experimental group participants were encouraged to make decisions for themselves. Langer (1989) wrote:

> Those in the experimental group were emphatically encouraged to make more decisions for themselves. We tried to come up with decisions that mattered and at the same time would not disturb the staff. For example, these residents were asked to choose where to receive visitors: inside the home or outdoors, in their rooms, in the dining room, in the lounge, and

so on. They were also told that a movie would be shown the next week on Thursday and Friday and that they should decide whether they wanted to see it and, if so, when. In addition to choices of this sort, residents in the experimental group were each given a houseplant to care for. They were to choose when and how much to water the plants, whether to put them in the window or to shield them from too much sun, and so forth. (p. 82)

Effects were dramatic. Three weeks after the experiment ended, residents in the experimental group participated more in activities, were happier and were more alert. Eighteen months later, 30% of the residents in the comparison group had died, but only 15% in the experimental group. Not unexpectedly, the relationship that was found between control and survival for nursing home residents mirrors our finding of how aggression and magical coping are associated with intact survivorship for those entering homes: Clearly, what is lethal for the very old is passivity and the lack of a sense of control, of autonomy and of mastery.

Thus, residents-to-be must not, if at all possible, be permitted to be passive and without control. In discharge, planning when in the process of relocation to a nursing home, residents-to-be must be encouraged to participate in decision-making on their own behalf and even if unrealistic, to believe they are in control.

At admission, staff must determine how best to structure the new resident's institutional life to enhance control. At Drexel Home, an initial treatment plan was developed based on the resident's characteristic way of coping and how the self is preserved. Over the years, we became rather creative. One example was providing the newly admitted paranoid resident with a roommate who was a "paranee," someone whose sense of self includes being critical of others. In turn, whenever a resident could be placed with a roommate who needed to nurture a more dependent partner the marriage was made. We were not, however, always successful. Jerome Hammerman, a director of the Home, liked to tell the story of a new resident, a gentle and soft speaking man, who timidly asked if he could talk to him for a few minutes. "Mr. Hammerman," he said, "you know you might have a nice home here but how can you give an old man like me a man to live with. I only lived with a woman, my wife, for over sixty years."

Assuring successful passage through the phase of the first month syndrome can often be difficult. Adverse effects must be acknowledged. Indeed my test of an inadequate (or, if you will, lying) administrator is to ask how residents adjust initially. If the response is "They do fine," I become suspicious. Confusion and depression is to be expected initially, but by the end of one month or so, with assistance from staff, the resident can be expected to reestablish a sense of self-sameness, albeit with underlying feelings of being a patient among the old, sick people and being closer to death. Still, these underlying feelings can be readily contained by a sense of control, as is the case in nursing homes with high quality psychosocial environments. Some ways to promote these kinds of institutional environments will be covered in the next section on working with staff.

WORKING WITH STAFF

An institutional orientation to enhancing residents' functioning must penetrate interactions between residents and staff at all levels. Such penetrations occur through staff's understanding of residents' behavior, but there are many barriers that must be overcome if there is to be accurate appraisals of behaviors, particularly of demented residents. Staff, like family, find it difficult to understand how seemingly pathological processes are actually functional. Aggressiveness, nastiness and even paranoid behaviors can, as has been shown, facilitate for adaptation to stress. Staff must learn to understand, tolerate and even nurture verbally abusive aggressive and paranoid behaviors directed at them by residents. Obviously, this is a difficult task, a task too difficult for some staff. It is also a task that is not assumed by staff in many facilities where even the most minor of deviations from ideal compliance and gratefulness are not tolerated.

Tolerating Deviancy

An illustration of intolerance of the nonideal resident was provided by a graduate social work student who selected to write-up, for an assignment in a course on psychopathology, a 67-year-old woman who resided in a nursing home. The student in his fifties, a minister whose newly self-appointed ministry was to work with, and for, the elderly, prepared an excellent case report.

Mrs. Green, who was recovering from a stroke, was always self-centered and impulsive. She had, for example, abandoned two children, one with each of two husbands that she left. A third husband had died within the past two years. Most accurately diagnosed as having a narcissistic character disorder, the student voiced his concern that Mrs. Green was labeled as "a histrionic who is always manipulating and demanding." His concern was that staff members were vilifying this lady rather than providing her with the care and attention she needed for her recovery. When I asked the student to describe Mrs. Green as a person, he became flustered and responded that she is self-centered but then added that "That is no reason to treat her so badly," "So," I asked "is the judgment of the staff wrong?" He was unwilling to accept, at this time, that there was agreement in the diagnosis and continued to focus on her bad treatment. After returning to Mrs. Green in the next three class sessions, it became apparent that the diagnosis was correct and that Mrs. Green was neither an admirable woman nor particularly likeable. Moreover, he began to realize that the task of the staff, and especially his task because he was not Mrs. Green's caseworker, was to help her in being who she is. It was not love she needed, and indeed he could not love her, but he could help her to retain her persistent self-centered identity.

As he became more open in discussing his feelings with his supervisor, it became apparent to him that although she too disliked Mrs. Green, she was able to accept Mrs. Green for the person she is and, also, to assist staff to do the same.

In this instance, some staff were sufficiently professional and mature to accept Mrs. Green's distasteful behavior. It would have been more difficult if Mrs. Green was verbally abusive rather than self-aggrandizing and demanding of attention. Similarly, staff must learn that magical thinking of residents can also be functional for adaption and survival.

Understanding Meanings of Behavior

Yet entry level staff cannot begin to understand the meanings of these seemingly pathological behaviors unless senior professionals do. Professionals however, can too easily interpret facilitatory processes as psychopathological if they use models developed for younger persons. We are taught that "good coping necessitates realistic appraisals" of one's capacities and that abusive behavior toward others reflects "bad object relations." Although such generalizations may generally be correct, they may be completely wrong when applied to the very old, particularly when they are under duress.

Staff must learn that bizarre behaviors often have meanings related to the striving for preservation of self. Once this principle is understood it becomes increasingly possible to see continuity between bizarre behavior and pre-morbid personality traits. In turn, as the bizarre behaviors become intelligible, staff can tolerate, or even encourage, seemingly aberrant behaviors that help the patient be him or herself.

Staff Frustrations

It is not easy for staff to be objective. They have, as Dobrof (1983) noted, good reasons for feeling angry, helpless and demoralized, frustrated and even betrayed. Feelings of anger toward residents is reflected in comments such as "How can he say these things to me? After all I have done for him?" Anger toward the family may be justified in a comment such as "Don't they even care about that old man? He probably just sits there like that because they never visit him." Thoughts about the other staff members and supervisors include "They leave all the dirty work for me. Nobody ever shows any appreciation around here." Feelings of helplessness and demoralization are reflected in "it doesn't seem to matter what we do, they never get any better." Should not the aide feel frustrated when saying to herself "I must have explained that to her six times already." The terrible feeling of betrayal is captured by the comment "After everything I have done for her, she doesn't even know who I am." There is obviously no easy way to reduce these painful feelings. Necessary, however, is to provide a sense of efficacy to the hands-on staff.

Managing Residents with Cognitive Impairments

Burnside (1981), a nurse with experience in long-term settings, in synthesizing techniques for managing patients with cognitive impairments, divided these techniques into three categories: techniques for the helper, specifically for memory development, and for manipulation of the environment. Her "bedside" helper techniques include reinforcing reality, using touch, supporting denial if it is therapeutic, and helping clients to express feelings. Reducing duress is particularly important. Situations that provoke agitation, including most new situations, must be recognized. Obviously, when the resident cannot communicate the source of the agitation, disorganized and aberrant behavior is likely to escalate. Staff education in communication is indeed very helpful. Can, in turn, staff become more comfortable and more competent, and feel more efficacious in working with demented patients? Certainly our observations at Drexel Home were that it is possible to enhance staff's functioning and feelings but only by support and reassurance of the more professional staff. The more staff are expected to put out, the more nourishment staff must be provided.

Regarding Burnside's ideas for retention of memory, she has provided a list that is appropriate for reality orientation groups, as well as recommendations for interaction outside of groups. For example, she suggests providing sufficient cues to aid memory and orientation (e.g., props to indicate change of seasons), consistent cues that encourage recognition instead of recall, and multiple cues; avoiding pressure to perform; being sure to communicate what is expected to be remembered; and being sure that familiar objects that reaffirm the continuity of the sense of self are on display.

Environmental manipulations are rather obvious such as using a night light; bright colors and decoration, color-coded doors, keeping the same staff working with individuals, providing a safe environment, that is not too boring but no over stimulating, a nonthreatening environment, providing clocks and calendars, and making special efforts to provide a milieu that reduces sundowner's syndrome.

BEHAVIORAL INTERVENTIONS

In vogue now are behavioral interventions. What is meant by behavioral approaches to intervention? Simply stated, interaction between the resident and the environment is first analyzed for factors that encourage dysfunctional behavior; then, new kinds of interactions are substituted that encourage restoration of ADL (activities of daily living) functioning; and, lastly, improvement in ADL is charted (see, e.g., Pinkston et al., 1982). Different terminology, however, is used by behaviorists; environmental contingencies that reinforce dysfunctional behavior are analyzed; new contingencies introduced; and targeted behavior charted for extinction of dysfunctional aspects and for increased frequency of functional aspects. Regardless of language, successful restoration of functioning has been demonstrated for a diversity of deficits including an inability to use eating utensils by use of one-to-one skill training at every meal; daytime urinary incontinence for wheelchair-bound residents by use of a bell and then toileting at a fixed two hour or so interval; and incoherent speech by constant positive reinforcement of intelligible speech and negative reinforcement (ignoring) unintelligible speech.

Need for Prosthetic Environments

If the successes are so impressive, why have behavioral approaches not been embraced with enthusiasm? Even under the best of circumstances as, for example, in facilities of high quality and with excellent training of staff to be the behavioral modifiers, improvements do not continue beyond the period of intervention. In the language of behaviorism: Unless prosthetic environments are developed to reinforce desired behaviors, reestablished functioning will decay and previously extinguished behaviors return (see, e.g., Lindsley, 1964).

A related reason for not maintaining effects is that too often a graduate student in psychology, social work or nursing has applied the intervention. Thus, he or she has devoted a great deal of time to an individual resident while providing relief for overburdened staff who invariably are delighted to have the added assistance. The presence of eager graduate students is indeed immensely valuable for improving morale and performance on units of cognitively impaired residents. This was certainly so on the unit where the doctoral student applied a behavioral approach to helping residents to empty their bladders on a fixed schedule. During the period he was on the unit, morale was noticeably better. Staff liked that affable student who was always courteous and respectful, and also, was most willing to lend a hand when called upon, for example, to help lift a resident or to carry a tray. In turn, only through their assistance to him, was he able to show that a bell that rang on a fixed schedule followed by the staff assisting the resident to urinate successfully kept residents dry. When he left, however, the staff felt an emptiness and soon reverted to letting residents become incontinent during the day.

Targeting Dysfunctional Behavior

A most important lesson from behavioral interventions is that unless appropriate levels of reinforcement are maintained, both outside of the minutes or even hours in a formal program, and beyond a fixed period of weeks and even months, improvements do not persist. But probably the most important lesson is that unless staff members are taught why what they are doing is particularly helpful to the resident, there is no generalization. When teaching staff the reason for interventions, they are being provided not only with the prerequisite knowledge for their actions but they are also receiving support, the necessary nourishment, for the arduous tasks of caring for cognitively impaired residents. Unless nourished, burnout quickly occurs. One kind of knowledge that too frequently is not the focus of behaviorists analysis is that the identification of dysfunctional behavior that necessitates change must be based on the purpose of the behavior for the individual. To reiterate once again, a behavior that appears grossly dysfunctional, and therefore a most appropriate behavior to change, may indeed be a behavior that is most needed by the resident because it is most critical for the preservation of self.

A poignant example occurred at Drexel Home when a trainee in behavioral interventions wished to change the fondling behavior of Mrs. Lewis, a quite confused female resident.

A confused resident, Mrs. Lewis, was fondling the breasts and genitalia of other women; this was particularly offensive to staff members. Psychiatrist Grunes had explained to select staff members that Mrs. Lewis' fondling was a reflection of the relationship with her deceased husband. Her daughter had related how her parents were such a loving couple that they always held hands and were constantly touching and gently petting each other. Mrs. Lewis was actually rather terrified of men and thus sought out women to replace her lost and needed tactile contact. Grunes' approach was to let her form a tactile relationship with a woman who appreciated Mrs. Lewis' attention and to confine the fondling, as much as possible, to secluded areas in the facility. Had the fondling behavior been extinguished, it was believed, Mrs. Lewis' deterioration would have rapidly accelerated.

Behavioral interventions must not be targeted on behaviors that preserve the self but, rather, behaviors that diminish the self must be targeted for change. For reinforcement to be effective, procedures must be incorporated into the service plan and be part of everyday routines. Implementation must be by staff who, whether as members of Nursing, Occupational Therapy, or Social Service departments, assure the creation of a prosthetic environment for each resident.

Successful Program

Using these principles, a behaviorally oriented psychogeriatric program was developed by Mallya and Fitz (1987) for serving up to two hundred residents in nursing homes, by using therapeutic assistants who provided hands-on behavioral interventions. The therapeutic assistants implemented an individualized treatment plan developed by a team of social work technical supervisors, an occupational therapist, psychiatric nurse and social worker; the clinical director was who a psychiatrist; a training director; and a program director. Facility support included consultation to administrative staff and training sessions with staff on topics such as aging, mental illness, communication skills, behavior management, medication management, the rehabilitation process, the therapeutic environment and family relationships. In these sessions, staff were encouraged to discuss psychiatric issues as they related to specific problems of residents. Delivery of treatment, in turn, included discussions of barriers to the resident's rehabilitation, treatment plan development, implementation, and assessment of outcome. They also implemented an outreach program to families which included monthly appraisals of their members' progress in treatment, communicated an understanding of the members problems, and encouraged residents to write letters to their family thanking them for visits, gifts and so forth. Therapeutic assistants conducted ongoing individual and group sessions whereas technical supervisors provided individual counseling and led life skill groups. Every three months, they and other team members reassessed the treatment plan and made modifications as necessary.

A preliminary assessment of impressions by staff who were not working with clients they evaluated revealed an improvement in 78% of their clients as compared to 14% for a control group. Improvements were perceived for their clients in reality orientation, activity participation, verbalization and socialization, ambulation, bathing self, dressing self, personal hygiene and continence. Although the apparent success of this behavioral oriented program, the hourly service cost ($21.60) may be greater then reimbursements permit. Despite the cost being absorbed by the project, some nursing home administrators did not participate because they feared a loss of control to an outside agency, particularly from the requirement of service providers to report substandard care and any action that could be abuse or neglect. This resistance to participation precipitated the purchase by Project Adopt of a nursing home where the same administration would be responsible for nursing care and psychogeriatric restorative services, not unlike in the best of contemporary long-term care facilities.

Structural Change

Beyond these kinds of behavioral-oriented programs that include modifying service plans that encompass implementation by aides, other innovations can be considered. A Wander-Proof Lounge, for example, was developed at the Long Beach Memorial Home in Long Island, New York, for wanderers who spent two hours per day in the lounge participating in structured programs and where they could roam freely and, also, provide a needed respite for floor staff (McGrowder-Linn & Bhatt, 1988). The lounge becomes a stable environment in which the wanderers can freely explore many artifacts of interest. Purposeful behavior is encouraged, and even aggressive purposeful behavior and, additionally, participants are urged to reminisce and form coherent images and expressions of the past, mechanisms discussed earlier as adaptive components of the unique psychology of the very old. When participants return to their floor, there is less random wandering and better sleeping at night.

STRUCTURAL APPROACH TO FAMILIES

What about the feelings of family members? By the time a decision is made to institutionalize an elderly member, the family often feels relieved but not without feelings of guilt and inadequacy and, moreover with great rage; that is, rage at oneself for being inadequate and rage toward the elderly person for inducing feelings of inadequacy. Too often workers focus on the family's feelings of guilt, rather than on the accompanying feelings of inadequacy and rage, as well as sense of relief, after institutionalization. Given this mixture of painful feelings, it is expected the reassurances of competent care by staff would be welcomed by families; and also welcomed would be subtle, and not so subtle, messages that it is not necessary to visit so much. It is indeed painful to visit a mother who is quickly deteriorating and may not recognize you. Visits by family members, however, are particularly important because of the effects of becoming institutionalized when old.

Helping Families to Visit

When an elderly person is institutionalized in a long term setting, the potentially deselfing process can be attenuated, in part, by interaction with family members. One common example is the importance of family visits to the seemingly intractably confused elderly resident of an institution. The elderly person may seem to be totally unaware of the family visitor at the time of the visit. Shortly after the visit, however, the elderly resident may become quite agitated, reflecting an awareness at some level of the visit often organized reminiscence replaces psychotic like ramblings. Albeit the importance to the resident, the visit can be quite upsetting to the family visitor and serve only to heighten the previously discussed feeling of guilt, impotence and rage. Unless some one explains to the family the specific meaningfulness of the visit, the family may reduce their visiting which can be quite harmful to the elderly resident.

A project was developed at the Jewish Home and Hospital for the Aged in New York to enhance communication between families and residents, particularly for family members of confused residents. Initially for families it has been expanded to staff. Project CONNECT (Communication Need Not Ever Stop) included a series of lectures and small discussion groups (Marchico-Greenfield, 1986). In addition to Burnside's suggestions, participants were encouraged, for example, to not, if possible, speak for the resident; include the resident in all discussions; give the resident choices and facilitate all decisions, be a good listener; and allow for reminiscing. These techniques, prepared for families, are precisely those that must be encouraged among staff.

For those without family, or families who are unable or unwilling to visit, a deselfing process can accelerate. Not only are these residents without the benefit of significant others who can reinforce the self but, also, staff are less likely to see the resident as a real person. For these residents who are without families, volunteers can be used who commit themselves to continual visits to the same resident. Most often through careful preparation and pairing, visiting persisted over a long time period.

Constant and persistent efforts must be made to educate family and staff. Some efforts must be continual, occurring in both formal regular staff meetings or in informal supervision of staff. Other efforts are sporadic as family group meetings which usually are held for families of newly admitted residents. Occasionally, there are special programs, as when family groups are convened to learn how to communicate with their impaired residents, or assisting aides in relating to families. A teaching program for aides can be developed so they know, for example, to whom specific complaints could be referred rather than accepting the blame of family members and becoming resentful, bitter and angry toward the family and the resident. The turnover of aides, however, makes this kind of penetrating time-consuming training difficult to maintain.

Deploying Staff for Family Interaction

Because family meetings are not sufficient to increase, and sometimes to even maintain, visiting, a more ambitious structural change can be implemented that consists of assigning a half-time worker to each unit of forty or so residents. Of critical importance, however, is the reorientation of staff to the families of residents. Workers should be selected and trained to be perceived by family members as all-loving and all-giving caregivers to their elderly family member resident and, in turn, administrative staff encouraged to let themselves be targets for hostile expressions by family members regarding the dereliction of the Home in caring for their relatives.

Family Visits to Mentally Impaired Residents

The best of homes, always encourages family visiting. As with many homes, however, as the residential population becomes more impaired mentally, there is a tendency for lessened visiting of family members. Attempts to maintain visiting patterns through family groups, such as family members of new residents, keep families involved in the home. Yet, as Safford (1980) found, members of more confused residents participate in these groups but do not necessarily visit either the floor of their resident family members or the resident her or himself. In withdrawing from interaction with deteriorating residents, some family members simply deny that their visiting has lessened while others become terribly upset with themselves and their inability to tolerate the deterioration, and still others vociferously blame the home for causing the deterioration. Common to families is displacing the anger toward themselves and toward the resident onto the home.

The extreme pain in passively watching the deterioration of a loved one is quite evident. As noted earlier, families welcomed relief from their psychological pain through being encouraged not to visit. Occasionally, of course, family members should not be encouraged to visit if it is too upsetting to them or to the resident. Surely, however, a general discouragement of family visiting can be a great relief to families but certainly dysfunctional for residents in reducing the maintenance of their identities and diminishing the perception of their uniqueness by staff. Thus, a task is to develop an approach to families that encourages their presence on residents' floors and, also, encourages face-to-face contact with even the most intractably confused family member.

Visiting as Helpful to Later Mourning

Another kind of observation is important to developing a structural approach. That is, those family members who continued to visit a slowly deteriorating resident until the time of death are less likely to have a protracted mourning process following the death of the resident. These family members, however, are not without feelings of inadequacy and rage during stages of deterioration. Thus, the approach must allow for displaced rage that we know can be beneficial for family members. It is better than rage turned inward causing heightened depression and, certainly better than rage expressed toward the resident. Aggressiveness by residents, expressed by staff in such terms as "complaining" and "griping," and sometimes as "bitchiness," should be perceived as facilitating adaptation and, when absent, cause for alarm. Unless complaining is tolerated, or even encouraged, staff become complacent and administrative needs outweigh resident needs.

Institutional Transference

From another perspective, an institutional relationship, or transference, is developed by families that includes both positive and negative projections. The home, that is, becomes both the life-sustaining all-giving other and, also, the life-impeding other that is the cause of the present, as well as further, deterioration in their family member. To direct this institutional transference into usefulness for the resident, a structured approach to the institutional psychosocial environment can be developed in which a "split transference" occurs wherein a unit worker becomes the all-giving, all-loving other, and administrative personnel the life-impending others.

The hiring of the unit workers is indeed a careful process in which persons are sought who were genuinely altruistic and giving individuals. With the unit worker, family members discuss the concrete needs of the resident. When, for example, a cherished 40-year-old thread worn and torn sweater is missing, the unit worker assures a family member who is totally convinced that it was stolen or lost in the laundry that every means is to be taken to recover it. Often, of course, the confused resident has misplaced it, or, at other times, the ancient garment had simply dissolved in the process of being cleaned and had been replaced by housekeeping with a sweater in better repair. After the worker's assurance, the family can leave the home knowing that the worker devotes herself, or himself, to searching for the missing cherished sweater. The sense of personal inadequacy and guilt thus become, in part, alleviated through projection onto the worker of feelings and actions of unconditional caring and loving for the family member in the home.

Family and the Worker

The psychodynamics in the relationship between family member and worker is indeed complex. This relationship does not exist during the process of becoming institutionalized when the resident-to-be feels abandoned and the family members feel they are abandoning a loved one. The resident-to-be must repress or suppress feelings of abandonment and focus on how the home will assure survival, as well as provide opportunities for activities and socializing with peers. If the older person does not respond passively to the current situation and impending institutionalizations, and also transforms the relocation into a voluntary decision and the home into a rather ideal environment for meeting needs, intact survivorship will be facilitated. In turn, family members must also be assured that "It's time to live in a nursing home." By placement in a facility of excellent quality, guilt becomes assuaged and staff of the home, particularly intake social workers, are perceived as assuring that the correct decision for placement has been made and that the home will appropriately respond to their elderly family member's needs.

After admission, however, families observe in their member, who is now a resident of the home, the vicissitudes of the first-month syndrome. The first-month syndrome, as noted earlier, refers to the marked deterioration manifested during the first weeks after admission by lucid residents. Some become extremely depressed, some very anxious, others quite agitated and still others frankly psychotic. Most new residents rebound from the first month syndrome by six weeks or so after admission and have recovered a sense of self. Modest changes from preadmission include some greater amount of hopelessness as well as greater preoccupations with illness and body. During this early postadmission phase, relief from caregiving is joined by the home becoming perceived by families as more impersonal in its caring than when accepted for admission. The family member, in turn, becomes observed as only one of many sick and deteriorating elderly for whom the Home provides care.

Transference to the Worker

Into this disillusioning process, the BA-level worker is inserted so that fantasies of the home's special concern and caring for "my husband," "my wife," "my mother," "my father," "my aunt," "my uncle," "my grandma," or "my grandpa" becomes reestablished. The worker is perceived as different from all other workers in the home. He or she is perceived as taking a special interest in the family member. For most, the rationalization for the special interest, concern, and care by the worker is because "mama after all is a special person," even when mama may actually only be a shell of her former self and not very lucid. A concurrent rationalization is that "I am a special person because of all I have done for mama." Thus the worker is perceived as an extension of self who is not unlike an ideal family member. The projection, at a less than conscious level, may be that the family-like worker loves mother in such a way that the attention and caring is from unconditional love and, certainly, not because it is paid employment. Indeed, for some family members the worker becomes the perfect child whereas as the daughter herself is the imperfect one. Thus there is a sense of satisfaction that mother's needs are being met with tender loving care.

Splitting of the Transference

Rage displaced toward the home may subside somewhat but it is not completely extinguished. The worker can assist in containing the rage through her or his own actions and, also, through explanations regarding how good the home truly is. Yet the displaced rage never subsides completely because the anger towards oneself for abandoning mother never dissolves, nor toward mother for evoking feelings of inadequacy, shame and guilt. The rage does not become directed toward the all-loving and all-caring worker but rather toward an authority figure: the charge nurse, the chief of social service, the associate director or the executive director can become the "bad" other who is causing all their woes. The covert feelings about these authority figures is that "if they only cared enough, they would make her well again." Such projections often have taken the form of irrational tirades, particularly when a symbiotic relationship exists between daughter and mother. If the professional judgment is that interaction between daughter and mother is helpful for the maintenance of the mother's sense of self-identity such verbal abuses of staff become tolerable. The staff can learn to understand and to appreciate that the irrational abuse is an expression of the daughter's internal state, particularly her own fear of personal dissolution, when observing deterioration in her mother. This is not an easy task! It can only be accomplished if staff themselves are supported and nourished by administration so that they can withstand personal abuse.

Success of the Program

Although a formal evaluation of the program was not undertaken, there was a consensus among all levels of staff that the restructuring was a great improvement. The long tradition of centralized social services and activity programs increasingly made less sense as the residential population deteriorated. More activities on floors lessened the burden of floor staff but, however, did not lessen anguish and anger of families. The presence and responsibilities of the BA level worker who not only discussed the status and problems of their family member but incorporated them into the service plan and sometimes into assisting with caregiving. Emerging from the program was a projection how to help families have a successful visit with their family member.

A significant shift occurs over time from perceiving the Social Service Department as part of administration and separate from the daily care of all residents to perceiving the Department as intimately related to even the most tedious of nursing procedures. When the worker assumes responsibility for explaining to a daughter why mother was not bathed immediately on wetting her undergarments, and has to wait a short while for the aide who was then busy, all floor staff appreciate the assistance. Also appreciative are personnel in housekeeping and dietary services who formerly were approached by families primarily to be criticized. Interpretations by workers of the duties and concerns of these personnel led to a better relationship with families, as well as between these personnel and administrative staff.

With the apparent success of the program, those administrative staff who were the targets of criticism, and sometimes vociferous verbal abuse, by families were better able to tolerate these behaviors. Sharing of information among the workers and administrative staff leads to a sense of partnership in which each set of personnel perceives and understands their role in encouraging successful visiting and in humanizing care. Clearly, more families are involved with not only their resident family member but also more staff members of the home.

When Drexel Home closed in the fall of 1981, we had the opportunity to further examine the split transference. Most residents were transferred to a new facility but twenty two were relocated to a variety of other facilities, predominantly proprietary (for profit) nursing homes. Although the split transference was dissolved, we fortunately were able to retain Drexel Home's Chief of Social Services to ease the transition by remaining as the residents' case worker after relocation.

A Case of Split Transference

To illustrate the split transference, as well as one form of the transference after relocation, I have selected Judy Brown, a never married only child, age 48, whose 74-year-old mother, Mrs. Brown, had been a resident in Drexel Home for five years at the time of relocation.

Ten years before her mother, Mrs. Brown, entered the home, Judy became "the manager" for her parents because her mother began to manifest psychiatric symptoms and her father had several severe heart attacks. During this period she discovered that the bickering between her parents "was serious," particularly when her father told her about his resentment and anger toward his deteriorating wife with whom, he said, he was never happily married. Although this upset Judy, her real concern was that the mental deterioration evidenced in her mother at an early age was to also be her fate. This was only one reflection of their symbiotic relationship.

Regarding the admission process, Judy felt that familial problems had escalated, forcing her to place "mama" in Drexel Home. Her mother was hospitalized twice in the year before admission because she was hallucinating. Whereas the hospital staff was perceived as not helping her mother, the intake worker at the Home was described as "fabulous." Albeit the hallucinations, mama was talkative and "really had personality." Judy grossly idealizes the wonderfully competent and vivacious mother of her childhood, as well as her parents' marriage. After admission the mother's marvelous "personality" continued, but staff in the Home became objects not only of Judy's love but also of her rage. Shortly after admission two suitcases containing her mother's clothing disappeared and she searched in vain for them, directly confronting staff she felt should have been responsible either for their not being lost or for their recovery. Since then she has been fixated on her mother's clothing and was verbally abusive to staff when any article appeared missing. She said "It's my way of getting back at them."

Because of Mrs. Brown's many problems when she was admitted from the hospital, she was placed on the medical unit. There she received intensive individualized care and Judy now recollects that her relationship became less "tense" with her father because they could visit mama and could talk about how she was doing. Judy feels that she can not talk to her father about other things and that she is "remiss" in attending to her father in other ways. After a year on the floor, Judy felt that Cindy, the unit worker, cared deeply about her mother and was an extremely good worker.

Judy visited her mother both in the morning and in the evening four to six days a week. On the days when Judy was unable to come, her father would come. Cindy remembers Judy's visits. Judy wanted certain things done: mother's hands must be clean (she would check under the nails), the wheelchair must not be locked, and her general appearance must be good. Cindy reported that when Mrs. Brown had difficulty chewing and was changed from a regular diet to a pureed diet, Judy came in and, sobbing, said "Why wasn't I informed." Cindy says, "It was like she became a complete mess," but Cindy was supportive of Judy and feels that her requests were not out of line.

Cindy continues to have a relationship with Judy and recently visited Mrs. Brown with Judy in the nursing home to which she was relocated. Other staff, however, have a different perspective. The staff members remember Judy as keeping a notebook on mama, complaining about nearly everything. For example, she wanted to know when the catheter was irrigated every day, and she insisted that this be done even though it was explained to her that this would just introduce more chance of causing an infection. Judy wanted to look in the charts to make sure that this was being done and when staff refused, she became very angry.

After complaining to the nursing staff, Judy would go and complain to the Director of Nursing and to administrators. She also would call other residents' families and board members about such issues as missing laundry. Judy incessantly complained to the Director of the Home whom she viewed as incompetent and indifferent and confirms this by saying that she never saw him on the floor. Judy's conferences with him were inevitably clashes, where she would scream and yell. Judy was especially resentful toward him when Mrs. Brown fell down. Judy went to the Director to find out why she had been able to get out of the chair. Because of her abusive complaints, he left for home early with a splitting headache. Judy has never forgiven him for her mother's fall.

The nursing staff, in turn, complained that though Mrs. Brown was incontinent, Judy expected her always to be dressed just so, but that Judy for many years never bought any clothes for her mother, which meant that the staff would have to scour the unit to find extra clothes for her. The staff felt that it was intolerable that Judy would inspect things and want things to be just so when she was not providing any clothes.

On the other side, Judy became very involved at the Home. She was the volunteer photographer for the Home, she became the editor of the newsletter, she visited other residents and became interested in them, she became involved with concerned families which she felt provided "minor support to families," and she wrote letters when Cindy was transferred to another unit. Mr. Brown also was a volunteer. He was not the complainer in the family, although he reports that he agrees more should have been done for his wife. At one point he had a seizure in the dining room at the home and was sent home in a cab with an orderly and was well cared for. Judy wrote a very long letter of thanks, extolling, in particular, the social workers.

Over the course of Mrs. Brown's stay she became more wheelchair-bound, more aphasic, had periods of yelling, would strike others if disturbed, and was on psychotropic medications. Throughout, Judy had very profound doubts that enough was being done for her mother. It appears that besides checking for certain signs of physical care that were important to Judy, the close relationship with Cindy was important in helping Judy with her feelings. As Judy became upset when the home was closing and the residents were being moved, she began crying and stated, "That'll be me in 20 years." She then talked about how she treats some of the staff members like family but feels that no one will really be caring for her. Judy visualizes herself as being in a Home and not being cared for.

For Judy, the transference was split between Cindy and the administrative staff. Cindy, was and still is, always described as a "doer" rather than a talker

and when Cindy herself made a special trip to the laundry to find a missing be-
longing of her mother's even though it was not found, Judy was satisfied. Her
fantasy is that Cindy has feelings and attitudes that are identical to her own. Simultaneously, Judy always found reasons to complain loudly to nursing and administrative staff and during her visits to mama she sought out problems for
which to complain that enough was not being done for her mother. Objects of
this transference were expected to allow themselves to be chastised, humiliated
and punished without complaint or retaliation. The director consciously understood this but could not help but feel persecuted when Judy would call Board
members who, in turn, called the administrator at Home in the evening. He was
so much the focus of her rage that she unjustly blamed him for all the Home's
fiscal problems and its closing.

In the new Home, Judy visited her mother as frequently as before but she did
not complain to staff as she was accustomed to doing previously. She indeed
had reason to complain. At one visit she found feces under her mother's finger-
nails and her mother was now confined to her room. Judy, however, was acutely
aware that if she complained as abusively as she had done in the past, that she
would be at risk of having her discharged from the new home. Now the transference was split between the good new Home and the terrible old Home that
cast her and her mother adrift. Unfortunately, after the relocation there seemed
to be, if anything, an intensification of the conviction that she will become "senile" at a young age like her mother and that no one will care for her.

Nature of the Transference

Judy's transference to staff is not unlike the transference found in other
family members. The content of the transference varied but the form, a
split transference, split between unit workers and administrators, is
similar. This form of the transference to the institution occurred only because an environment was created that facilitated its development. In
turn, the rationale for creating a facilitory environment is based on clinical experience, particularly on the importance of family visiting in maintenance of the resident's sense of self and the psychodynamics of families in relation to institutionalized elderly members, as well as their
transference to the institution. Basic to the milieu developed is the handling of impotence and rage.

Observed also is the experience of impotence and rage in the case
worker who was retained to follow the 22 residents who were discharged primarily to proprietary nursing homes. After relocation, the
case worker experienced those feelings of impotence and rage that are
characteristic of families. These feelings of the case worker were handled by Grunes and myself, who remained as consultants, and were
also alleviated as the case worker used his expertise to help families and
to manipulate staff of the nursing home to provide individualized care

to former Drexel Home residents. Because the proprietary facilities tolerate little criticism of the care they give and, also, discourage visiting in ways that are not always subtle, the case worker often became a family surrogate maintaining an ongoing relationship with the former resident. Many family members have felt relieved in lessening their interactions and investment in the resident but generally with adverse consequences for the resident, both in terms of the ability of the resident to maintain a sense of self-identity and in the diminished personalization of the resident by staff.

What Have We Learned?

What have we learned from the Drexel Home experience? The therapeutic interventions for the very old residents have been guided by an understanding of psychodynamics and psychoanalytic theory. The interventions, however, were not carried out by psychoanalysts nor, at times, by persons sophisticated in psychodynamic theory or principles of psychoanalysis. Still, the encouragement of a split transference in families was of help to residents. Thus we need to consider a distinction between psychoanalytic interventions with the elderly that are undertaken by psychoanalytically trained professionals who use knowledge of the psychology of the latter half of life, and those interventions that are based on psychoanalytic principles and knowledge of the psychology of the latter half of life but are carried out by those who are not so trained or who are not even familiar with these principles and this knowledge.

The development of institutional environments that encourage a split transference by family members is a particularly good example because the staff of long-term care facilities are likely neither to be knowledgeable of psychodynamics of aging nor of psychoanalytic principles. Yet guided by this knowledge we may be able to facilitate the development of beneficial milieus that include educating some staff to become "all-caring" unit workers and other staff to accept the role as the target of frustration and anger. Investigations that demonstrate how to effectively use psychodynamic wisdom in long-term care facilities would add immeasurably to our current state of knowledge and would indeed be helpful to the elderly and their families.

Families are concerned with doing the "right thing" in the future for their elderly members when caregiving will be their responsibility. They need to know what they do matters; that is, that what they do can make a difference in the life of their elderly family member. Only through helping families to realize how they can make a difference can we have the necessary impact. To address this issue, Weinberg (1974) wrote a paper entitled "What Do I Say To My Mother When I Have Nothing To Say?" His message to professionals in this instance was to let children know that just by being there "you make a difference." Our research supports the importance of reassurance by "being there" as well as the importance of communicating to elderly family members that actions taken on his or her behalf will be in accord with personal wishes. Facilitating the communication of this message is knowledge of availability of specific services that will be helpful were a crisis to occur. Educating families in how to provide emotional security to, and thereby enhancing a sense of the continuity of self in, elderly members not only aids the older person but also provides assurance to potential and current caregivers that what they are doing is appropriate and meaningful. This assurance, in turn, can provide gratification in caregiving even when caregiving may be extremely onerous.

Satisfactions from caregiving are rarely discussed. The daughter who leaves the institution in tears because mother did not recognize her but became agitated when she left may never be told her visit was a meaningful one for her mother. When the worker explains the meaningfulness of the visit, it is possible for family members to understand that their presence helps in the retention of a sense of self. Needed, therefore, are approaches in long-term care that accept the painful feelings of families and build on their potential satisfactions as they remain in intimate contact with debilitating family members. To do so may necessitate structural changes within long-term care facilities and, certainly, education of staff to the meaningfulness of family interactions, as well as to the process of becoming institutionalized when old, to the unique psychology of the very old, and to personhood in advanced old age.

Chapter 6

Preserving the Self Through Religion

Churches and synagogues, and religious beliefs and practices, are of great importance to the current cohort of the very old who not only participate in formal religious activities but also pray, read the bible and watch religious television programs at home. Apparently, religiosity enhances well-being, and religious coping behaviors are used to deal with difficult experiences. Also, cherished religious possessions aid in maintaining and preserving the continuity of self. Moreover, as will also be discussed, to live until advanced old age is usually to feel personally blessed by God. Additionally, the belief in an afterlife is associated with reunions with deceased loved ones, which attenuates their loss and enhances current well-being. The meaningfulness of religion is most evident among those devout elderly persons who when homebound feel abandoned by church or synagogue. The chapter will end with a focus on enhancing the mental health preservation of the self through religion, especially through increasing collaboration between secular and sectarian sectors on behalf of old people.

RELIGION IS AGING

According to Riley and Foner (1968), who surveyed the literature through the mid-1960s, more than five of six persons 65 and over (86%) believe in the existence of God. Similarly, the Harris poll in the early 1970s (Harris et al., 1975) revealed that about 75% of those age 60 and over feel that religion is important in their lives. Church and synagogue attendance among the elderly further reflects the importance of religion in the lives of the elderly: The national poll also found that 80% of those 65 and over reported having been to church or synagogue in the previous two weeks. Since the 1970s, local and national polls have confirmed the extent of religiosity among the elderly.

The most recent Gallup poll (Gallup & Castelli, 1989) revealed that 9 of 10 Americans, independent of age, have never doubted the existence of God, 8 often say they believe that they will be called before God on Judgement Day to account for their sins, 8 in 10 believe that God still works miracles, and 7 in 10 believe in an afterlife. In all, 71% believe in an afterlife and only 16% do not. Belief in an afterlife is even high among the least actively religious group (58%) and highest among the most actively religious (81%). Although many religious beliefs decline with educational attainment, beliefs in an afterlife do not. Apparently, but not reported, beliefs in an afterlife are held by more than 71% of those persons who are in advanced old age.

Commenting on the importance of religious institutions for elderly people, Palmore (1980) has written:

> Churches and synagogues deserve special consideration because they are the single most pervasive community institution to which the elderly belong. All the other community institutions considered together, including senior citizen centers clubs for elders, unions, etc., do not involve as many elders as churches and synagogues. (p. 236).

Among the very old, however, attendance decreases. Some of the very old are too frail to attend services, whereas others do not have transportation or cannot climb the steps of the church or synagogue. There are some older people who say they "can't afford nice clothing" to go to services, and still others feel that younger members of the congregation have pushed them aside. Although attendance at formal worship decreases among the very old, personal religious practices, such as reading the Bible, prayer, and watching religious programs on television, are often maintained or even increased (Gray & Moberg, 1977).

Religiosity and Well-Being

In more homogenous groups of elderly people, associations have invariably been found between religiosity and well-being (by, e.g., Heisel & Faulkner, 1982, on urban Blacks; Koenig, Kuale, & Ferrel, 1988, on Christians in the Bible Belt; Markides, 1983, on Mexican-Americans). For these groups that have been assumed to be religious, well-being is related to the three kinds of indicators of religiosity, to church attendance, private practices and self-ratings of religiosity. Because relationships between indicators of religiosity and well-being are not found in heterogeneous sample, an interesting interpretation presents itself: Among those reared in a religious family, elderly persons who have remained religious have greater feelings of well-being than those who have not retained their religiosity. If this interpretation is correct, it supports the usefulness for the old of the retention of beliefs and practices from earliest life for preservation of the self, and for feelings of self-continuity and well-being.

Using Religion to Cope

Magical coping has been focused upon throughout this volume because of its widespread use among the elderly for dealing with age-associated losses. It was also recognized in Chapter 1 that it is a common and helpful way to cope with stressors that are independent of age such as cancer, as reflected in Taylor's (1989) "cognitive illusion."

When, however, people are asked about their perception of how they have coped with stressful events, an interesting picture emerges. Older people invariably introduce religious coping behaviors. Koenig, George, and Siegler (1988), for example, found that more religious coping behaviors were spontaneously introduced than non-religious coping behaviors when elderly respondents were queried about coping with difficult experiences. Nonreligious coping behaviors encompassed focusing attention on other activities, accepting the situation, and seeking support from family and friends. Among religious coping behaviors the most frequent was trust and faith in God, followed by prayer, help and strength from God, church friends, church activity, minister's help, read the bible, knowing it was the Lord's way and lived a Christian life. Although this study was conducted in the Bible Belt (the Durham, North Carolina area), religious coping behaviors appear to be quite prevalent throughout the country. For example, it has been common to assume that religious coping behaviors are characteristic of those only in the Bible Belt and among Blacks in general, but, when elderly people of varied backgrounds are encouraged to tell what has helped them deal with crises, prayer invariably is soon mentioned.

It is the personal, private religious coping activities that dominate, rather than the social or group-related dimension. That is, in the Koenig, George, and Siegler study, private prayer, faith or trust in God, and strength derived from God comprised nearly three-fourths of the religious coping behaviors mentioned. Thus, the benefits from religious coping are, apparently, less from church and synagogue social activities, or from clergy, and apparently more from a sense of control through faith. For those who have little control over their lives, or for those in a situation in which they have no control, magical beliefs in control are helpful. Magical beliefs can be non-religious cognitive illusions of personal powers or religious faith in which the appraisal of danger is diminished ("God would not do that to me") or the assistance received will help overcome the danger ("God will see me through").

Religious Possessions

Valued personal possessions are particularly important for maintaining continuity with the past (e.g., Csikszentmihaly & Rochberg-Halton, 1981; Kamptner, 1989; Sherman & Newman, 1977/78). Cherished or treasured personal possessions encompass photographs, jewelry, art work and also religious items As noted by Kamptner (1989), these kinds of personal possessions

> may assist individuals in maintaining and preserving their identities in the face of events that erode their sense of self; they may trigger and enhance the life review process; and they may represent ties or bonds with others at a time of life when social losses tend to be greatest. (p. 182)

It is quite understandable why religious icons and artifacts are prevalent in the homes of the elderly, particularly bibles and prayer books that have given a lifetime of use. One elderly Jewish woman said, "I still keep my husband's tallis (prayer shawl) as if he will come through the door and run off with it to shull to daven (synagogue to pray)."

BLESSED BY GOD

When the book of Proverbs was written, few people lived to 70, "three score and ten," then the demarcation for advanced old age. Infant mortality was high, women died in childbirth and epidemics wiped off large segments of the populations. Rare were those blessed with old age. Thus the orientation to time and one's life course was appreciably different. Delaying until tomorrow what could be done today was not sensible if death was ubiquitous regardless of age.

Only recently is a large percentage of our population living until advanced age. The mortality curve is becoming "squared." That is, when chronological age is plotted against the percentage of persons alive, it is apparent that an extraordinary percentage are alive at each age until a rather sudden drop off in the later years. Expectations have thus become the living out of one's life course, for example, to not only seeing grandchildren but also great grandchildren and even great great grandchildren. Delaying gratifications and events, such as marriage and childbearing becomes understandable if people perceive themselves to have many years to live.

Then, in turn, when old, the self-fulfilling prophecy comes to pass. An anticipated life course has been lived. Having lived a long life it becomes possible to declare that life has been lived as it should have been lived, as "I have been raised to live my life." Given that most Americans are religious and believe in a personal relationship with God, it becomes understandable why so many also feel personally blessed. The Old Testament certainly provides ample support because late life is one of God's blessings (Psalm 91:16, and also Proverbs 9:11) and longevity is a reward for prior service (Deuteronomy 4:40). Often quoted is: "A hoary head is a crown of glory; it is gained in a righteous life" (Proverbs 16:31).

Making Life Meaningful

Besides being a passive recipient of God's blessings when old, it is possible to consider growth through, according to LeFevre (1984), "the individuals making sense that there is meaning of life" (p. 3). The making of life meaningful to oneself is a life-long task that takes on different dimensions when age-associated losses occur and as the awareness of nonbeing becomes most real. Beyond sustaining and maintaining oneself, and therefore one's sense of meaning to self and others, is the possibility for new meanings from a reassessment of one's life and goals, and then placing one's life in perspective in preparing for death. The waning of our power toward the end of the life can possibly facilitate a reassessment in which conventional values of mastery and control become of less importance; it may facilitate a realization of one's interdependence with others, or one's place in the continuity of generations, of one's uniqueness and possibly, a consciousness of making meaning of one's whole life (Snyder, 1981).

REUNIONS IN THE AFTERLIFE

Another kind of personal blessing is embodied in reunions with loved ones in the afterlife. The meaningfulness of reunions was illustrated by Mr. Poulin:

Mr. Poulin, an 87-year-old retired autobody welder of French Canadian descent, lost his wife, Suzanne, four years ago. Because they married when he was 17 and Suzanne 16, they had been married 66 years at the time of her death. He maintains a close relationship with his two daughters, both who live nearby and visit on weekends. During the week he socializes with cronies in his public housing complex and volunteers with the Little Sisters of the Poor three days a week. Still, he feels very lonely when he thinks about Suzanne and "the good times we had together." He then added, "But I have friends here, so I don't get very depressed." Now somewhat choked up, he continued by commenting that he especially enjoys his occasional trips to churches and shrines in Canada. A few minutes later when asked what death means to him, he lightened up, smiled and answered, "I am ready whenever the good Lord calls me. It will be good to get back with Suzanne and the rest of the family."

Mr. Poulin's picture of the afterlife is obviously not of sitting on a heavenly cloud strumming a harp. Rather, it is of being surrounded by loved ones and especially for Mr. Poulin, being reunited with his beloved wife of 66 years, Suzanne. Reunions take many forms. A lonely 83-year-old woman who has been widowed for 22 years has a shrine in her living room for her dog Rufus who died 8 months ago and whom she raised from a puppy. A leash hangs from the shrine and as she talks, she glances over to the shrine and says, "Whenever I get too lonely, I stroke the leash. I'm looking forward to seeing Rufus again." She never mentioned reunions with her parents or her deceased husband but only with Rufus, her lone companion for the past 8 years.

Reunion fantasies are also evident during the phase preceding death when cognitive decline can be found. As will be discussed in the next chapter on accepting death, some elderly respondents gave "happy-magical" responses to queries regarding what death means to them. My interpretation of these kinds of responses of something happy and magical in death is that they reflect the anticipation of reunions with departed loves ones.

Reunion fantasies following death of meaningful others is surely helpful to the mourning process independent of age. Still, as Mr. Poulin illustrates, the belief in reunion can be accompanied by the simultaneous grief from the loss, which also can occur at any age. Indeed, there is no evidence that mourning is either harder or easier among the very old. Mourning, however, often appears easier among the very old but it is not because of the mourner's age nor because of the age of the deceased, a wife for example. Rather, when it appears easier, it is likely to be a function of the grief work accomplished, "anticipated grief" when the death of a loved one has been a slow process. In these instances, by the time death occurs, it may even be welcomed by the person who dies, as well as the mourner.

A difference, however, between young and old mourners is the apparent susceptibility of mourners in their advanced years to react to grief with greater morbidity and even mortality (Parkes, 1973). As discussed in previous chapters, because of older peoples' limited homeostatic reserve, an adverse reaction to a severe stress can lead to a downward course that can eventuate in a hastening of death.

LOSS OF CONTINUITY

The meaning of religion in preservation of the self is possibly revealed most clearly among those who feel a loss of continuity with their religious past. In our work on the church as service provider (Tobin, Ellor & Anderson-Ray, 1986), one focus has been on those who are partial shut-ins or are complete shut-ins. Mrs. Cohen, a partial shut-in, illustrates feelings of being abandoned by her church that are indeed painful for her:

Mrs. Cohen, an 81-year-old widow with "heart problems," lives alone in subsidized housing on a limited income. Without family nearby, she would like someone to drive her to synagogue and to assist her up the stairs. She added that she is unhappy that people she met at her synagogue have not visited. "No one has called except the rabbi . . . I don't know many people, but I did belong to the sisterhood, and they know I'm sick."

Shut-ins may not expect assistance to attend church and synagogue, but they do expect home visits. One of the oldest ways that churches and synagogues have addressed the needs of the elderly is through their ministries to the sick and shut-in. Mandated both by biblical and institutional traditions, home visitation has taken place for thousands of years and continues in religious congregations today. Indeed, visitation remains the cornerstone of ministries to the homebound. Prayer at home and watching religious programs on television do not always provide the kind of continuity needed to preserve her meaningful religious identity. A bright and articulate woman expressed this problem as "not connected enough with my church and my God."

It's Changed, Not Me

And then there are the very old individuals who have aged in one place only to find that their church has changed and their minister has departed. As one respondent noted, "It seems I'm still the same, but it's changed; you know, church, minister, old friends." She, however, is fortunate because she is able to retain her faith by reading religious magazines especially the Bible, listening to religious programs on television and radio, and praying privately. She is indeed different from many others who are unable to retain their religious identity if not physically attending services Still she is dealing with feelings of being abandoned by her church.

In Nursing Homes

Because of the importance of religion to the current cohort of elderly people, nursing homes in some states are required by law to assure that their residents have an opportunity to practice their faith. To better understand the types of religious activities which are currently being provided in nursing homes, a study was initiated of seventy one nursing homes in the Chicago metropolitan area (see Tobin, Ellor, & Anderson-Ray, 1986). As part of this survey, a staff person at 20 of these nursing homes was questioned about their religious programming.

The survey revealed that nearly all nursing homes provided some type of regular religious programming. On the average, these nursing homes provided four to five religious programs which were held on a weekly, biweekly, monthly, or seasonal basis. Many homes offered services for residents of differing denominational backgrounds, including Roman Catholic, Protestant, and Jewish services. Community clergy led these services in 75% of the homes, with nursing home staff and lay people occasionally leading services. Residents rarely participated in leading their religious services. Clergy made regular visits to residents in three-fourths of these homes. Only about half of the homes, however, provided special holiday programs, as well as Bible studies for residents.

Although impressed with how many churches and synagogues were providing a variety of programs in nursing homes, the study also raised some concerns about how adequately the spiritual needs of residents were being met. First, were concerns about the quality and appropriateness of religious programs offered in nursing homes. A poorly organized and weak program is quite ineffective. Second, it was very difficult to judge whether programs were properly matched to the needs and interests of the residents, particularly because all residents must be given an opportunity to observe religious practices which are part of their belief system and religious heritage. Yet, not all homes mentioned programs which were designed for their residents of varying denominations. Most homes do not restrict their intake to only one religious group. Found was that many homes provide ecumenical worship services or a single Protestant service to meet the needs of many of their residents, but these services were rarely accompanied by additional services for specific Protestant denominations, Roman Catholics, and Jews. This approach to programming creates a variety of problems.

A single ecumenical service or generic Protestant service rarely is able to meet the needs of all residents because it does not allow residents an opportunity to worship in a manner that is consistent with their denominational guidelines and traditions. Not all Protestants will enjoy the same Protestant services. Nor will all Catholics be satisfied with the same mass or all Jews accept the same "Kiddush" service. But of most importance, is that unfamiliar rituals are not best for facilitating the preservation of self. A sensitive response to spiritual needs requires providing each resident with a range of options for worship and allowing the resident to choose to participate in observances which are most consistent with his or her personal faith and religious traditions.

Making available a wide range of options in worship means more than providing several different types of worship services. A diversity of programs can be designed to address spiritual needs in nursing homes. Opportunities to participate in group prayer services, choirs, or musical groups and study groups are of interest to some residents. Regularly receiving the sacraments is important to most Christian residents, while other ritual observances are important to Jewish residents. Special worship services which are planned to fall on the high holy day are terribly important for residents, yet special holiday services are not held in all nursing homes.

More individualized programs can be of great value to residents. Visitation and distribution of the sacraments are the most common of these individualized programs. For many residents these provide an extremely important opportunity to address their spiritual issues and needs, as well as to observe important religious practices. A variety of other programs may be developed, ranging from a pastoral counseling program to a telephone or card ministry. Allowing residents time and a private prayer and mediation is also very important. Helpful, too, are religious icons in the daily living environment. Nurturing religious identities can indeed facilitate a preservation of the self.

SECULAR-SECTARIAN COLLABORATION

Because the importance of religious beliefs and practices can never be minimized, especially for the current cohort of the elderly, the worker or therapist must be attuned to how each person's religious beliefs and practices maintains and preserves the self. Additionally, there must be a sensitivity to how religion is used in coping with crises. Much has been written on religious aspects of work with individuals and their families. Given, however, inadequate attention to collaboration between secular and religious sectors, a synopsis of our work in this area may be instructive (see Tobin, Ellor, & Anderson-Ray, 1986).

In Different Worlds

Steinitz (1980) in her study of the churches and social service agencies in one community, found that clergy and human social service personnel rarely collaborated in service provisions to the elderly, even though they often worked with the same people. She quotes comments by administrators of social service agencies about churches. The Director of a local Commission on Aging said, "My mind doesn't include churches" (pp. 138–139). This sentiment was echoed by the Director of a Senior Center, "Contacts with churches are, at best, incidental. We don't think about them" (pp. 138–139). The senior attorney of a legal assistance project stated: "No one on our staff is very religious, goes to church. We don't include churches in our work with seniors" (pp. 138–139). Clergy expressed similar feelings about social service agencies. The minister of a Methodist church reported: "I hardly ever get asked about agencies in the community." At best, the Steinitz data suggest that the clergy and social service agency directors know very little about each other. Clearly, this can be dysfunctional for the elderly. For example, there are times when it is appropriate to refer an elderly person to a pastor or rabbi for counseling, and also there are times when the elderly person should be referred to a social agency.

Barriers

Possibly the greatest barrier to working together is a lack of communications which results in many misconceptions about each other. Unfortunately, work demands of clergy and social service agency personnel make it difficult to spend the necessary time for appropriate introductions. Then attitudes and personalities of professionals can interfere. In one community we studied, the only major community social service agency for the elderly was directed by a person who wanted everyone to work together but to do it only that agency's way. Although clergy felt working with that agency could be helpful to the needs of their aged, they had so many negative encounters with the director that they were unwilling to do so. While we would like to believe that the personality of professionals is not a factor in any consideration of working together, in reality, it can be a significant problem.

Examples are also found where working together was inhibited because of differences in values. Clergy who do not believe in abortion do not send anyone to social service agencies that condone abortions. In one community, clergy at opposite ends of the theological scale were the ones most opposed to working together. At one extreme, the conservative or fundamentalist Christian clergy felt that Jesus was the answer to everything and that even the other churches would not understand this enough to justify working with them. At the other extreme, the Unitarian Universalists found it difficult to work with some other churches because they continually discussed God, and god is not a necessary part of the Unitarian philosophy. In like manner, Jewish Orthodox and Reform congregations may find it difficult to work together. In turn, service personnel often believe that guilt causes undue anguish and perceive clergy as inducing guilt. Clearly, each church, synagogue and social service agency feels justified in its position, yet the potential for their elderly clients to miss out on the benefits of collaborative programming is significant.

Since 1980, the potential for working together has been explored by an increasing number of groups. For example, recognition of the highly personalized nature of volunteer caregivers to fellow church members has led the Robert Wood Johnson Foundation to fund interfaith coalitions to recruit, train, and supervise volunteers to provide home care to the frail elderly. Lebowitz and collaborators (Lebowitz, Light, & Bailey, 1987) have shown how coordination between an Area agency on Aging and a Community Mental Health Center (CMHC) led to an impressive increase in the caseload of elderly patients at the CMHC.

Our Model

To facilitate working together, we developed a model for increasing interaction among churches, synagogues and social agencies. The primary goals of this action program were to enhance the role of the church and synagogue in providing for the elderly, and to encourage interaction between religious congregations and social service on behalf of older people.

The first of the three phases focused on the development of a working relationship with a "lead agency" in each community. This lead agency served as a point of entry and base of operations in the community. In an effort to facilitate the development of the relationship with the lead agency and to support the efforts of the project, a project assistant was assigned to the lead agency. The role of this staff member was to act both as an advocate for the elderly and as a "neutral" person who could mediate between social service agencies and churches or synagogues by making contacts, suggesting ideas, and moderating disputes. Another important task during phase one was to develop better understanding of the community by making informal contacts and working with community leaders to establish strategies for future work.

The second phase started with a systematic survey of clergy in the community, using a standardized questionnaire. The interview questionnaire was designed to provide a profile of needs of the elderly as perceived by the clergy. Included in the survey were queries on current church-and-synagogue-sponsored program on gaps in services for the elderly, on ways to enable the elderly to participate in programs and help others, on barriers to collaborating, and on willingness to participate with other clergy and service personnel in developing services for the elderly. In addition to gathering useful information, the survey was designed to sensitize clergy to the needs of the elderly and to prompt consideration of alternative strategies for addressing those needs. In two communities, social service personnel were also interviewed. Further, an attempt was made to survey a small sample of elderly people in each community.

With the completion of the surveys, the third phase began. Survey results were compiled and presented at a meeting of clergy and social service agency representatives. After discussing the findings, plans for future activities were considered. In some cases, clergy asked for assistance with individual efforts in their churches, while others expressed interest in planning joint activities or program among churches, synagogues, and social service agencies. After this point, community leaders were expected to take the primary initiative in planning and developing programs, but the project staff remained available to provide consultation regarding program development and to support collaborative efforts.

Success in One Community

In one community, there was great success due largely to the commitment by the lead agency, a CMHC, to developing a positive rapport with clergy and supporting communitywide efforts to improve services for the elderly. About half the clergy in the community were able to be interviewed, most of whom were affiliated with Roman Catholic, Orthodox, and mainline Protestant churches,. There was a great deal of difficulty, however, contacting and interviewing clergy from the more fundamentalist and storefront churches. Personnel from all 12 of the identified social service agencies which served the elderly were interviewed.

The CMHC serves a large industrial area of 40,000, half of whom are people of color. One of five distinctly different communities served by the CMHC was selected, an urbanized heterogeneous low-income area (median per capita income of $6,499). Although the CMHC provides inpatient and many outpatient services, it has no specific program for the elderly. The director expressed interest in developing a working relationship with the churches in his service area, particularly regarding the elderly, and our Community Advocacy project was linked primarily to the Consultation and Education (C&E) Department.

The surveys, particularly of CMHC personnel, helped to increase awareness of issues and also developed curiosity about how their responses compared to others. Also revealed however, among other findings, was that referrals were uncommon and that there were many obstacles to collaboration, including the clergy's perception that CMHC personnel did not appreciate the role of religion in the lives of their clients and CMHC personnel's perceptions that clergy proselytize and are not trained to provide counseling.

Yet, a group of CMHC personnel, clergy, and staff from social service agencies who were in the surveys were willing to meet to discuss collaboration. The tone of the initial breakfast meeting was informal, and the discussion was lively. A number of ideas were suggested: such as a joint effort to provide preretirement and postretirement training for seniors, to develop life enrichment groups for seniors, to develop a comprehensive directory listing programs provided by social service agencies and churches, to invite clergy to participate in monthly family committee meetings, to discuss clergy visiting the CMHC jointly planned workshops, and to form a short-term task force to plan collaborative activities in the community.

A report containing the findings from the surveys was then mailed to all of the clergy and service providers who were unable to attend the community meeting. In the follow-up activities, CMHC exhibited willingness to carry through specific responsibilities, such as using project staff as consultants, working with a local senior center, developing the comprehensive directory, and beginning to develop a training program to help staff learn more about working with local clergy, and the CMHC also committed itself to work toward establishing new policies and procedures for working with clergy.

A task force composed of CMHC personnel, local clergy, and mental health professionals representing other community agencies then started meeting monthly to discuss a variety of theological and psychosocial issues as they related to counseling clients or parishioners. Discussions were lively and informative, focusing on the topic selected by the committee. Such topics as divorce, love and marriage, and helping people help themselves were included. Some discussion sessions opened with case presentations by either a therapist or clergyperson, and other sessions began with less formality. The group expressed ideas, perceptions, commonalities, and differences during six monthly meetings.

At the spring meeting, eight clergy and six mental health professionals evaluated their progress. The consensus was to discontinue the meetings during the summer months and to reconvene in the fall with a more structured agenda. One member suggested utilizing the expertise of individual committee members to learn from one another. Several training topics were suggested for the fall, including stress, how sacred writings can be used in counseling, therapy with the oppressed, black theology and pastoral counseling, grief and loss, counseling the elderly, the hospice movement, and abused older adults. Comments were very favorable, and additional types of coordinated efforts were mentioned, such as having therapists and clergy co-lead groups and having clergy refer their parishioners to groups offered at the CMHC. Clearly, CMHC personnel and clergy became aware of shared issues and showed an openness toward working together. Of significance is that during the one and one-half years of the project, by the end of the summer, referrals of elderly to the CMHC increased from two to 17.

FINAL COMMENT

Religious institutions, which are particularly important for the current cohort of the very old, are likely to be of less importance for future cohorts. Still, because the United States is the most religious of advanced technological societies, religious institutions will continue to be important for preservation of the self. Possibly for more than any other group, Black elderly people of lower socioeconomic status are members of churches that provide not only spiritual well-being and solace but the kind of interpersonal connectedness that cushions the precarious safety net of their lives and also provides them with family-like supporting others that are not kin. The importance of fellow church members who become persistent life-sustaining significant others can not be underestimated (see, e.g., Gibson, 1986; Kulys & Tobin, 1980; Taylor, 1986; Taylor & Chatters, 1986). This kind of mutual support may, in part, be from necessity but it surely offers a special benefit lacking in the lives of many elderly persons and it certainly is an aid to preservation of the self.

Chapter **7**

Acceptance of Death

Death becomes acceptable at the end of life when the perception is that a life course has been lived and that there is no unfinished business. To live long, as discussed in the previous chapter on religion in the preservation of the self, is felt by many to be personally blessed by God. Concurrently, a shift occurs from a concern with nonbeing to a concern with the process of dying, and to the wish not to die in pain, confused or alone. The decline in cognitive abilities preceding death at an advanced age (the so called "terminal drop") is unaccompanied by preoccupations with, and fears of, death. However, for those with unfinished business because of being in a transitional situation, such as in the process of becoming institutionalized, anxieties about death are likely to accompany the phase of terminal drop, a phase that may have begun more than a year before death itself. In addition to the group that cannot accept death because of situational unfinished business, two other groups will be discussed, those with responsibilities such as elderly parents of disabled adult offsprings for whom they are providing a home, and those with self-assigned life goals such as artists who are still striving to express their visions. To be sure, there are other elderly individuals who can not accept their own deaths for these, as well as other, reasons. There are those, for example, with unfulfilled expectations emanating from unresolved life-long conflicts. Given the heterogeneity of the elderly, the chapter ends with the question: What is the future of accepting death?

CAN DEATH REALLY BE ACCEPTED?

Apparently, only humans are aware of their own death, of their own nonbeing. And possibly, as Kierkegaard (1844) has noted, it is not possible to escape from the dread of death.

A Personal Comment

I am fearful of death. In common with all human beings, I know my life will end and, probably in common with others, I suppress thoughts of my nonbeing as much as possible. Given my dread of nonbeing, when we, Morton A. Lieberman and I, launched our longitudinal studies of relocation of elderly persons, now over two decades ago, we avoided asking elderly respondents about death. Reinforcing our decision was the reluctance of interviewers to query older respondents about their impending death. Typical comments made by the interviewers, all professional women in their forties who were selected, in part, because of good relationships with their own parents, were, "They will clam up and tell us nothing afterwards," and, "If I have some questions on death at the end of an interview session, they will be so upset that they will never talk to me again." For the interviewers, as well as for me, to uncover attitudes toward this dreaded and suppressed topic would be disastrous for the respondents and for the study.

But then we discovered that our respondents invariably introduced the topic of death. Indeed it was the rare respondent who did not mention that he or she was near death, and also that non-being was less feared than the process of dying. Fears expressed, tended not to be of death itself but rather fears related to the fear of the process of dying.

First Evidence

Although I was familiar with Munnichs' (1966) then recent seminal work in which he had reported an acceptance of death among elderly persons in the Netherlands, I was disbelieving of his results. Munnichs had written:

> It was extremely surprising to us at the time that there was a great preponderance of confidence and lack of apprehension, though more than half of the number of persons interrogated admitted that they did think about the matter. We realized this unexpected result was that if death was awesome in character for only few exceptions, the field of experience during old age must be of a different nature from what is generally supposed. (p. 12)

"How," I asked myself, "could a person of any age accept his or her death?" Because, however, our findings confirmed his findings, I had to confront the inescapable truth. Whereas I can do so intellectually, deep down I still harbor disbelief. It probably cannot be otherwise among those of us in our middle years. But at least we can make the attempt to understand why it is that towards the end of life the very old can accept their nonbeing.

Implications from Death Becoming Acceptable

This topic is of concern not only because of its significance for life span theory and clinical practice with the elderly but also for social welfare and health policies in an aging society. Daniel Callahan (1987), an ethicist in his middle years, has argued, for example, that because of limited health resources, the elderly must be willing to forego costly life sustaining medical care. They must be convinced that it is best for future generations, and for our society as a whole, to acquiesce to rationing so that resources can be deflected to the young. But if death is acceptable at the end of life, it is not costly medical care that is wanted. Rather it is caring that will ease the process of dying. Is this not similar to Saunder's reasoning when, in 1967, she developed the first modern hospice? Acute medical care, including costly heroic measures, recedes in importance when what is wished for is the best death possible.

Interest in Death

Our study of the psychology of death among elderly people occurred at a point when the topic almost became a preoccupation among social scientists, mental health experts, physicians, theologians, and humanists. This preoccupation was evidenced at meetings of national professional and scientific organizations, which were incomplete without a symposium on death and dying. The burgeoning social science literature on the topic ranged from investigations of attitudes toward death to inquiries into the social context of dying to broader concerns with how the mortality of human beings constitutes an existential crisis. Most recently, a concern has been on the ethics of letting people die.

Death in the Psychology of Aging

At the time of our, really Lieberman's, initial excursion into the study of death and dying when very old, a special kinship was felt with some of the then recent explorers of the psychology of death. We, as they, believed that the study of death becomes a way of understanding aging. Erikson (1950), for example, in calling attention to human development throughout the life span, reflects this shared interest in the psychological role of death at the end of life. The speculation of Butler (1963) that the awareness of the nearness of death evokes a life review and the work of Cumming and Henry (1961), which is based on the assumption that disengagement is a consequence of this awareness, similarly reflect the theme that old age must be understood in terms of how individuals cope with their approaching death. In his pioneering study, Munnichs (1966) succinctly sums up this point of view.

> When we ask ourselves what are the most characteristic features of old age, one difference, compared with other periods of life, stands out most prominently, namely the fact that there is no other period following old age. . . . The experience of death, that is to say, to realize and to know that life comes to an end, and adjustment to this fact, might possibly be considered as the focal point of the mentality of the aged. (p. 4)

The studying of death began with Munnichs' assumption that the elderly know their life is nearing an end and must confront the psychological reality of their own finitude. Although social scientists may have long ignored this reality, it is not a topic ignored by elderly people themselves, nor is it a topic that older people dread discussing.

MEANINGS OF DEATH

Death can hold a variety of meanings for both the young and old. In describing attitudes toward death, Shneidman (1973) observed that death is "the most mysterious, the most threatening, and the most tantalizing of all human phenomena" (p. 3). Death can be feared, yet also accepted, dreaded but welcomed. Death can mean loss, change, conflict, and suffering, but it can also mean triumph (see, e.g., Davidson, 1975). Each person is challenged to unravel the meaning of death in a highly individualized manner. Attitudes toward life, previous experiences with death, and the specific circumstances surrounding death will shape a person's reaction to a death.

Because human beings are the only creatures known to be aware of their own death, some theoreticians and theologians have made the awareness of death the basic principle of human existence. In turn, every culture has developed ways of helping its people to cope with this quality of existence to facilitate mourning and to limit an extended mourning process. Indeed, belief system and rituals are indispensable for dealing with the apparent innate fear of dying. Thus all cultures must provide a system of beliefs to explain death. In some cultures, the meaning revolves around an afterlife. In others, the focus is more on living through one's children and the belief that the family and social institutions that have been left behind will endure following death.

Cultures also vary in the way they define events that are worse than one's personal death. In Oriental societies, for example, loss of face may be more painful than the thought of personal nonexistence. Also, dying to save one's children or dying in defense of one's country has become acceptable for most people is most societies. For the very old, it is not uncommon to wish "not to suffer anymore," and therefore death is welcomed.

Death as Loss

In our culture, death is most often perceived as a loss. Feifel (1977), in synthesizing his findings from studies of conscious and unconscious attitudes toward death, concluded that the unconscious fear (in his words, "outright aversion") is defended against by limited fear and ambivalent attitudes. This pattern, he maintains, allows "us to maintain communal associations and yet organize our resources to contend with oncoming death" (p. 10). Becker (1973), on the other hand, when dying at a young age, focused on the denial of death (the title of his book) through positive illusions and magical coping; for example, through how imposing logic and order onto the world assists in the denial of the randomness of death.

Although death in our culture is perceived as loss, perceptions of what is lost varies. One survey (Diggory & Rothman, 1961) surveyed people and found that seven kinds of losses were associated with the contemplation of death:

1. Loss of ability to have experiences.
2. Loss of ability to predict subsequent events (e.g., life after death)
3. Loss of body and fear of what will happen to the body
4. Loss of ability to care for dependents
5. Loss suffered by friends and family (e.g., causing grief for others)
6. Loss of opportunity to continue plans and projects, and
7. Loss of being in a relatively stable state.

Concern Among the Old

It was found that the greatest concern for men was their inability to care for dependents, whereas the greatest concern for women was causing grief to family and friends. Persons between 15 and 39 selected causing grief to friends as their major anticipated loss through death, whereas those over 40 chose the inability to care for dependents. In a later study, when Kalish and Reynolds (1976) included more people over 55, they found that caring for dependents was less important for this age group. What was important for elderly people was not a concern with future plans, nor death itself, but concerns with having no control over how they will die, concern with not dying alone, and fear of dying with pain. Others have also noted that older people fear death less than younger persons.

Divine Reward

The fear of death itself is often projected onto the very old by those in the middle years. Kastenbaum (1975) has conjectured that it is functional to do so because thoughts of an untimely, off-time, death are especially painful. Indeed, whereas people of advanced age can be perceived as having lived a full life, death at an early age can only be perceived as being cheated of life. Some actually feel that death at a relatively young age is a punishment for not having lived a good life. If, however, one lives to old age, it is often assumed that the person has lived a moral life and that old age has been given as a "divine reward." According to Simmons (1945), the Hopi believed that kindness, good thoughts and peace of mind lead to a long life; and among the Berber, deceit was punished by a shorter life. So too, as discussed in the previous chapter, most Americans feel personally blessed by God if they live to an advanced age.

Concern is with the Dying Process

Whereas elderly people think of death more often than do younger persons, the thoughts are usually about the process. With the increased prevalence of Alzheimer's disease, thoughts of confusion before death have been added to concerns about control, pain and aloneness. There are further practical concerns, such as the making of funeral arrangements, living wills and durable powers of attorney.

DYING WHEN OLD

Becoming "old," discussed in Chapter 1, is akin to Marshall's (1975) "anticipated finitude" because it is related to age but also to other factors such as the ages at which family members have died; and also to Keith's (1981–82) finding that, in addition to chronological age, the transition was related to health status for women and the presence of family members for men. Although the transition to becoming "old" is to be aware of the nearness of death, it is not necessarily associated with considering oneself as dying. Dying refers to a terminal period when it is assumed that life is now ending, that death is imminent. For this period, Kübler-Ross (1969) has postulated a series of stages independent of the age of the dying person:

STAGE 1: *Denial.* First reactions when aware of impending death may be denial, shock, and disbelief. Denial is a defense which allows an individual time to slowly adjust to the thought of dying.

STAGE 2: *Anger.* After a period of denial, the dying individual often becomes angry and asks, "Why me?" Anger is often directed at family, friends and caregivers.

STAGE 3: *Bargaining.* In this stage, the patient wants more time and asks for favors to postpone death. The bargaining may be carried out with the physician, family, or more frequently, with God.

STAGE 4: *Depression.* Depression is a signal that the dying person has begun to accept impending death. Illness can no longer be denied, as it causes greater weakness and pain.

STAGE 5: *Acceptance.* If younger people reach this stage, death is accepted. Although essentially devoid of feeling, he or she wishes to be close to loved ones, but verbal communication may be unnecessary.

Observations of many other thanatologists have confirmed the experience of these sequential feelings among the young when they are dying. There is, however, considerable disagreement as to whether or not dying individuals generally experience the full range of feelings or in the sequence of stages she detailed, particularly among older people who can more readily accept their own death. Shneidman (1973) suggests an alternative conceptualization. In his work with younger people who are dying, he has observed that their feelings can be described as a "hive of affect, in which there is a constant coming and going (of feel-ings)." He further characterized the emotional stages of the dying when young as

> a constant interplay between disbelieve and hope, and against these as background, a waxing and waning of anguish, terror, acquiescence and surrender, rage and envy, disinterest and ennui, pretense, taunting and daring and even yearning for death—all in the context of bewilderment and pain. (p. 7).

According to Shneidman, there is not a single, constant movement through stages but vacillation between acceptance and denial. Kubler-Ross also has cautioned that not all people will experience dying by go-ing through each stage in an orderly fashion.

Differences Among People

The value of comparing formulations is that it provides a slightly differ-ent view of the types of feelings any dying person may experience. Caution must be given not to infer that any one of these views presents a portrait of how people die. Each individual faces his or her death in a unique way. There is no single way to die, much less an ideal way to come to accept death. The person who feels that death is to be raged against and does so with his or her last gasp, is actually dying the way in which he or she wishes. Another individual may become more re-signed and passive, approaching death in a peaceful manner, as noted by Cato, in Cicero's (44 B.C.) essay, "De Senectute," ("On Old Age"), a section of which was reproduced in Chapter 1; recall,

> There had to be a time of withering, of readiness to fall, like the ripeness which comes to the fruits of the trees and of the earth. But a wise man will face this prospect with resignation, for resistance against nature is as pointless as the battles of the giants against the gods? (pp. 214–215)

We are, unfortunately, not all so wise. Rather, an appropriate death is dying the way the person chooses and not necessarily with a sense of equanimity that we as bystanders may wish.

What is Important Now?

Perhaps, the central question in working with the dying is: What is im-portant now? To answer this question, it is essential to identify the immediate needs of the individual and family, and respond to these needs. Careful timing of responses is also important, since many dying individuals often have limited energy to deal with the world around them. Separating the issues of dying from those of death itself can also be useful for both the dying individual and those providing care. Fears about death, its unknown aspects, and questions of existence or nonexistence are related but somewhat different from those of the dying process. There may be a wish, for example, to attend the oncoming marriage of a favorite great granddaughter. It is not uncommon among those of us who work with the very old to have observed how death is delayed until after participation in a welcomed event. Waning residual energies are mobilized for the event and then, afterwards, there is a giving in to death itself. Saunders (1969) has referred to this time of giving in to death, to the time when there is an awareness that death is imminent, as the "moment of truth." In common with persons of younger ages who have suffered a protracted terminal period of dying, many people who die at an advanced age can apparently accept the "moment of truth."

Inescapable Anxiety?

Still, as with me, there may be covert, suppressed and repressed, fears. Freud, for example, suffered until the end of his life from death anxiety. Becker (1973) wrote: "I don't believe that the complex symbol of death is ever absent, no matter how much vitality and sustainment a person has" (p. 22). But, of course, it was Kierkegaard who introduced us to the existential paradox, that of "individuality within finitude." Whereas each of us has an identity that transcends the natural order of species survival, never can we transcend our personal demise. This dualism of the human condition is the price we must pay for being human. According to Kierkegaard (1844), in becoming human, our consciousness creates the dread, the anxiety regarding our nonbeing. It is only human beings that have this peculiar and greatest anxiety. If so, how is this anxiety managed during the process of dying in advanced old age?

TERMINAL DROP

There is a phase when death occurs at the end of life, that has been referred to as "terminal drop," which more accurately should be called something like "the phase of terminal cognitive deterioration." Kleemier in 1961 reported observations of intellectual changes in an aged population as early as two years prior to death. Since then many other investigators have substantiated deterioration in intellectual functioning before death. These observations were recalled by Morton Lieberman when an aide in a nursing home to which he was a consultant was able to predict which residents were on a terminal course. Her explanation for her powers was because of her ability to pick up their "brain waves."

Exploratory Study

Ignoring this obvious correct explanation for her powers, he designed an exploratory study to determine whether systematic changes in ego functioning and emotional states occur in elderly persons prior to death and, if they do, to differentiate such changes from changes associated with nonterminal illness. (For a fuller exposition on this exploration, as well as the next two that will be only briefly discussed here, see Lieberman & Tobin, 1983.) For this exploration, a small group of institutionalized elderly were administered brief tests at frequent intervals. Those who died within one year of the last testing (a death-near group) were compared to those who lived for at least one more year (a death-far group).

The death-near respondents showed a pattern of declining performance over time on the tests of cognitive functioning. In contrast, the death-far group showed a pattern of improving performance over time, apparently a result of practice effects; that is, increasing familiarity with the test. Both groups were similar on measures of affects. But examiners' notes indicated that the death-near group made more spontaneous comments about something being wrong or something "going on" or, at times, referring explicitly to the realization that they were going to die. Generally, however, depressive content was not more characteristic of death-near than death-far respondents; nor did the content analysis of test responses reveal increased anxiety or fear. Finally, the performance of death-far individuals who became ill and recovered revealed that illness per se could not explain the decline of performance found in the death-near group.

Why the Decline. Before death, respondents showed decreases in level of organization but changes in affect were not systematically related to approaching death. Possibly the observed psychological changes preceding death are best viewed in terms of the individual's decreased ability to cope adequately with external demands. Perhaps the aged person approaching death experiences upheaval because of currently active disorganizing mental processes, rather than because he or she fears approaching death. The observed psychological disintegration may not be a reaction to the unknowable, but may rather represent a general decline of the system preceding death, as reflected in the variety of physiological and psychological measures. If this interpretation is correct, some frequently reported phenomena in the terminal phase of life become more understandable. In turn, many observers commented on the psychological withdrawal of the dying patient and have suggested that the withdrawal is functional because it protects the individual from intense separation anxiety. Suggested, however, is that withdrawal represents an attempt to cope with the experience of inner disintegration. Individuals approaching death pull away from those around them, not because of a preoccupation with themselves, but because they are engaged in an attempt to hold themselves together; that is, to reduce the experience of chaos and retain a sense of self.

Symbolization of Death. Because the changes examined in this explanation were primarily alterations in functioning, the task set for the next exploration was the examination of symbolic processes, comparing those nearer and those further from death to determine if awareness of death played a role in the observed psychological changes. Some marginal evidence from the respondents studied suggested this as a plausible direction. Many of the elderly we studied sensed some type of change and felt it to be different from that of illness. The labeling of the subjective experience, however, varied with some respondents reporting only a vague sense of feeling "different," whereas others said that they were going to die soon. Comments such as these suggest that more thorough and sensitive phenomenological reports would be a useful avenue for research in the terminal phase of life.

Second Exploratory Study

Next the focus shifted to studying emotional life when death is approaching. For this exploration respondents from the longitudinal study of the process of becoming institutionalized were used. In all, there were 172 respondents: 100 interviewed for 12 to 16 hours in four to six sessions while on waiting lists to enter homes for the aged (of whom 85 actually entered the homes), 35 in a matched community sample, and

37 in a sample of persons who were residents of the homes for one to three years. Of the 172, 40 had died within twelve months. These 40 were paired with 40 who survived an average of three years beyond the last interview session. Matching was based on a hierarchical sequence of comparison criteria: living arrangement, gender, age, birthplace, marital status, and educational level.

Neither Depression nor Anxiety. Significant differences in cognitive functioning, orientation to emotional life, and self-image were found between matched pairs. These findings substantiated the results of the previous exploration, in which impending death was found to be associated with cognitive decline. Most important was the finding regarding affects, not affect states per se, but rather, orientation to emotional life. Those closer to death are apparently not more depressed, nor have more anxiety, as is frequently reported in clinical papers, but they do avoid introspection. The magnitude and consistency of differences on measures of orientation to emotional life suggests that this finding is not an artifact and that those approaching death are unwilling, or possibly unable, to look inward because at some level of consciousness they recognize their impending death. It is as if they avoid introspection because of the fear of what they might discover. Although the nature of this monitoring process is unclear, the pattern of findings does indeed suggest a reduction in introspection without necessarily a modification in type or intensity of affect per se. Despite the almost universal focus of the psychological literature on the association of proximity to death with anxiety and withdrawal from others, these data, including impressions of the interviewer, did not reveal this association.

Toward Dependency and Affiliation. Another finding from the matched-pair design suggests a slight but measurable shift in the content of self-concept, away from assertiveness in interpersonal interactions and toward dependency and affiliation or, in the language of Bakan (1966), away from agentic aspects and toward communion. Although Bakan's concepts of agency and communion represent a higher level of abstraction than was revealed in our assessment of self-concept, his application of these constructs in relationship to Freud's concept of death instinct offers a framework for explaining the apparent modification in self-concept and is consistent with the findings from the analysis of death symbols discussed shortly.

Preoccupation and Fear of Death. All direct statements related to death that respondents made in the interviews were collated for both groups, and the responses for each person were typed on a card without identi-

fying information. The raw data, then, consisted of 80 paragraphs com-
piling all statements each respondent had made about death. Two
scales that could be reliably rated were developed to discriminate individual differences; a three-point scale rating degree of preoccupation
with one's own death and a four-point scale of fear of death. Inspection
of the distribution for these scales showed low preoccupation and low
fear for approximately forty percent of the death-near group, suggesting
either that the sensitivity of these scales was poor or that the phenomenon tapped by these measures applied only to a subsample of those
near death. Further analysis was required to determine the significance
of the large number of death-near individuals who did not respond as
anticipated on these two scales. Perhaps the low degree of introspection
previously noted as characteristic of those close to death was an important influence. Many of these individuals may have been unable to discuss their thoughts about death and dying directly. This possibility led
us to develop measures less amenable to the respondent's conscious
control.

Death Symbols. Responses were analyzed to a set of institutional TAT
cards developed by Lieberman and Lakin (1963). Four types of symbols
were analyzed: first, direct references to death and dying such as struggling to save one's life in drawing; second, issues of rebirth; third, in-
scrutable events or mysterious trips; and fourth, death figures or the
specter of death, such as a figure with hands folded or face covered.
Then the eighty respondents were rated for the presence or absence of
one or more of the death symbols for each TAT response. The results of
this blind analysis indicated that death symbols were rated as present
for 34 of the 40 death-near respondents and for only nine of the 40
death-far controls. Thus, although spontaneous comments did not reveal extensive preoccupations and fears, projective data did reveal that
symbolization of death occurs among these closer to death. To what extent these symbols intrude into consciousness cannot be determined
with any specificity.

Third Exploration

In a third exploration, 41 death-near respondents were compared to 41
matched death-far respondents from among 386 community residents
who were participating in a longitudinal study. The findings replicated
those from the earlier explorations. Added, however, were queries on
how they envisioned their death.

Happy-Magical Responses. The two groups differed significantly in how they envisioned their deaths. The death-near showed a much higher proportion of "happy-magical" responses and "concern about suffering" responses than the death-far group. Death-near and death-far groups were about equally divided in the response categories of "natural process," "denial," and "finalism." The death-far group held an almost exclusive claim on the categories of "traditional religiosity" and "mystery." Of interest is that the near death group was responsible for 77% of the happy-magical responses, which reflect a sense of personal urgency and almost desperate conviction that something happy, pleasurable, and good is waiting for them after death. Although not revealed by these data, it is my speculation that these were the more religious respondents whose vision of the afterlife was reunion with now deceased beloved persons. Invariably when asked to talk about their afterlife, believers discuss reunions, a topic discussed in the previous chapter on religion in the preservation of the self.

Interpretations of Findings

Deterioration in ego functioning with impending death can be explained as either the behavioral manifestations of central nervous system disorganization or as a reaction to disturbing affects caused by inner awareness of the disorganization. Probably both explanations are accurate. Evidence for a reactive process is found in the lessened propensity to introspection and the greater passivity when portraying the self in interaction with others among those closer to death. Both kinds of evidence suggest some active process in which painful underlying or latent meanings and affects are screened from consciousness. The success of this process is suggested by the inconsistent evidence for differences in emotional states between those nearer and those further from death. In the first two explorations, differences were not found in emotional states, whereas in the third exploration there was a modest association between depression and impending death but not between anxiety and impending death. There was also an increased prevalence of preoccupations with death and fears of death among death-near respondents in the second exploration. Because these preoccupations were neither intense nor ubiquitous, it appears that many if not most elderly people approaching death are able to contain the experience and thereby limit conscious pain.

Underlying Experience

What is the nature of the underlying experience of approaching death? The most consistent finding was that death-near respondents introduced symbols reflecting death when telling stories to TAT cards. What are the likely mechanisms of such symbols? As shown in the first study, acute illness crises, in which respondents recovered, did not produce such symbols. Neither did those who recovered from acute illnesses show the same pattern of decline as those who died soon thereafter. It seems equally unlikely that the signaling process was set off by self-detected changes related to decrements of aging—social and personal losses, physical incapacities, and the many onslaughts undermining self-image. Most if not all respondents had suffered multiple losses and physical decrements associated with advanced age. Nor did environmental setting generate such death symbols in those close to death. If environment influenced production of symbols, more institutionalized respondents should have shown death symbols inasmuch as the old-age home itself is sometimes perceived as symbolic of death; that is, as a "death house."

The kinds of symbols and losses introduced into projective responses suggest that a variety of meanings are attributed to an inner, possibly diffuse and ambiguous experience. For some, the meanings of the internal changes prodromal to death are narrowly focused on separation or bodily decay, while for others the meanings are not as specific, encompassing a sense of nonexistence itself. Despite the diversity of symbols employed to superimpose meaning on inner changes, the nature of the underlying psychological experience is probably the potential dissolution of the self. The presence of these covert meanings suggests the usefulness of an explanatory model that includes signal anxiety, the below conscious, latent or covert anxiety that Freud postulated as what is being defended against by defense mechanisms. An out-of-awareness experience of prodromal disorganization or disintegrative somatic changes is detected and experienced as a threat to the self, with subsequent signal anxiety. In response to the signal, the detected changes are symbolized and attempts are made to defend against the anxiety. Although depressive affect may be associated with such symbolization, manifest anxiety is not. Only through further study will it be possible to determine whether this absence of manifest anxiety is specific to the very old, who apparently are most accepting of their own finitude than are younger people. On the other hand, the elderly may be more likely than younger people to become cognitively disorganized in the absence of manifest anxiety because of a less efficient central nervous system.

The burden of defending against internal threat may overwhelm an already weakened ego.

UNFINISHED BUSINESS: SITUATIONAL

The lack of substantial evidence for manifest anxiety in the phase of terminal drop is not surprising if it is assumed that death is acceptable when on-time. With life tasks completed, elderly persons who consider themselves to be "old" are likely to be accepting of death and also not to respond to inner signals of impending death with fear. For those, however, who have unfinished business, impending death may indeed be cause of concern and manifest anxiety.

Thus, returning to the second exploration, differences in emotional life were compared between those who were undergoing the terminal drop phase in the unstable situation of being in the process of institutionalization to those in stable situations. Of the 40 matched pairs, 22 pairs were waiting to enter homes for the aged or had recently entered such homes (unstable environmental circumstance) and eighteen pairs had lived in the homes for the aged from one to three years or were living in the community (stable environmental circumstance). Next matched pairs were compared but now divided into two groups, to determine whether psychological processes associated with nearness to death differed depending on whether the respondent was in a transitional situation.

Preoccupation and Fear

The death-near respondents in unstable environmental circumstances showed more preoccupation and fear than the death-far respondents. No differences were found, however, in preoccupation and fear between death-near and death-far respondents in stable environmental circumstances. As noted earlier, approximately 40% of all death-near respondents had shown preoccupation and fear, and when the sample of pairs was divided between those in stable and unstable environmental circumstances, preoccupation and fear were characteristic mainly of those in unstable circumstances.

Death Symbols. Mr. Richards, a respondent in the death-near group who was in the unstable environmental circumstance of waiting to enter a home for the aged, introduced a variety of death symbols when telling stories to TAT cards. One example is his response to a roommate scene showing two elderly persons sitting across from each other on their beds carrying on a conversation:

Those two men are having a conversation. This fellow [left] is trying to convert him [right]. The old man on the right says, "I'm trying to change your opinion." Then he goes on to say, "You say you're going to live longer than Winston Churchill, but you're not." By the way, did you know I'm still waiting for the Messiah, Christian Messiah that is, has come, but we Jews have been waiting for the real Messiah for 5,000 years. I prophesy his coming.

Mr. Richards shared these kinds of death symbols and themes with death-near respondents independent of whether they were in the process of being relocated. The direct inquiry into his thoughts and feelings about death, however, revealed preoccupations and fears characteristic primarily of those in the process of being relocated; that is, in the unstable situation. To the sentence completion stem, "Death is . . . ," he responded:

I'll go to sleep [said bitterly]. I ain't so strong; weakest part is not being well. Death is nothing, just going to sleep. One hour is just another hour gone. Time means nothing. Everyone tries to plan, but it is impossible. No future. I don't think about things.

This response was scored high for preoccupation. And later in the interview he revealed his fears by associating his death with separation:

I'm better than many people. I prepare myself always. I even have the stone next to my wife. I told the children that if I possibly . . . the best thing is just to go. Each day goes by. Death is like a shot, when she died it was just like a shot. Time is gone. I plan ahead. Next year I'd like to go to europe, but I don't know if I can go. The future is the best thing if I have a companion. The future is to get a companion, go out together and not to lose one's mind.

Reworking Accepting Death

Symbols of death, therefore, were evident among those near-death independent of situation but whether the experience signaled by approaching death is contained, however, depends on the external situation. Environmental change constitutes a severe transition for the elderly: Previous patterns of relationships, meanings of significant others, and the self-image are challenged and tested by disruption of the environment. Individuals in the crisis state may have been more distressed and reactive over impending death but not, however, because their approaching death was of core concern but, rather, because life had again impinged on them, forcing them to make new adaptations and to face anew previously solved problems including, perhaps, a previous resolution of the meaning of their personal death. If death were the essential threat, rather than the life yet to be reorganized, more signs of avoidance, denial, or other similar psychological mechanisms would be expected in response to impending death.

UNFINISHED BUSINESS: RESPONSIBILITIES

Other elderly people have unfinished business because of responsibilities. One group, for example, are parents of mentally retarded offsprings who live with them. An example:

Mr. Newsome is a 77-year-old former chemical engineer who, except for part-time assistance from a paid home health aide, is the primary caregiver for both his 49 year-old profoundly retarded son and his 80-year-old wife who is a victim of Alzheimer's disease. Despite considering his own health to be good, as well as possessing a charming, erudite, and dapper demeanor, Mr. Newsome revealed awareness of his increasing frailty by his comment "I've become less sure of myself during the past three or four years, and more often I've been getting feelings of light headedness." Also, since the onset of his wife's Alzheimer's disease, Mr. Newsome's informal support network has been reduced to his brother and sister-in-law who telephone each night to check up on him; a niece who is "generally available" when needed; and a pastor who provides moral support. Although the concrete assistance provided by this support network is minimal, Mr. Newsome stated that "There seems to be more comfort in simply knowing that they are there if I need them." When asked if it would be best if other family members were to care for his son after death, Mr. Newsome replied "It's not fair to place the burden on them." He then commented about residential staff: "If motivated and caring enough, they could learn to care as well as me." When queried about what he enjoys most about caring for his son, Mr. Newsome very emotionally replied: "Just having him around, especially now that my wife is bedridden." However, when asked what he enjoys least about caring for his son, Mr. Newsome's rational and efficient approach as a former engineer became evident: "He's slow at meals, and consequently, it's late getting him to bed. So, I don't get much sleep at night, but I make up for it with catnaps during the day. You know I often wonder why I can't deal with this better, and that's very irritating to me!"

Indeed, the theme of regarding caregiving as a challenging problem waiting to be solved rationally permeated the interview with his inability to finalize plans regarding the future living arrangements of his son. Interestingly enough, although specific and comprehensive plans have been finalized regarding the guardianship and financial security of his son, Mr. Newsome does not seem able to take the steps necessary to put his son on a waiting list for a group home. When asked what has prevented him from doing so, Mr. Newsome replied in a downhearted and puzzled manner: "I don't know! I really don't know! Nothing I guess, I just have to get off my behind!"

Mr. Newsome clearly has unfinished business and although he is aware of his increasing frailty, suppresses thoughts of his death. Instead he focuses upon care for his wife and son, both of whom do need him. Because nobody can care for them as well as he, he is indeed in a quandary. It is better, he believes, to continue with the status quo, valiantly carrying out his responsibilities, than accepting his own death and contemplating future arrangements for his son, as well as his wife.

UNFINISHED BUSINESS: LIFE GOALS

For most men, as it is for Mr. Newsome's, life goals are encompassed by family and occupation, Freud's "Liebe und Arbeiten." Whereas Mr. Newsome's work goals were achieved, his goals for his family were unfulfilled because of his current responsibilities. Still, for both men and women, there may be unfulfilled family goals because, for example, of ambitions for children that have been thwarted. Whereas unfinished life goals are likely to be caused by disappointments and losses, they can also be caused by perceptions that time is too short to achieve self-assigned ambitions. Artists, for example, differ from most by remaining creative in aging and, also, like others who pursue the creative life, do not separate vocational from avocational pursuits. Indeed with age, as artists become mature and know the kinds of problems they wish to solve and how they wish to approach solving them, as Georges Braque said: "As you become older, art and life become the same."

Visual Artists

The drive to be creative was expressed loud and clear by 44 active artists over 70 in a 1987/88 traveling exhibit, Elders of the Tribe, organized by Bernice Steinbaum, who has a gallery in New York City. In turn, Connie Goldman produced a one-hour audio tape containing excerpts from interviews with the participating artists. In his interview, Will Barnet said: "No one should ever retire. It's an indignity to retire. I can't understand why anyone would retire. I get itchy fingers. What do you do with your hands." That is, what do you to with your time if you stop creating art? Louise Nevelson concurred: "I never thought to retire. I don't like vacations. I want to work. I feel alive when I work." Reuben Nakian at 86 echoed these sentiments: "If I don't create something every day I feel I have not done anything. So if at the end of the day I haven't done anything, a I sit down and make a sketch or two, just something." Nakian then added: "I feel like a twelve year old kid but with more experience and my bones ache more." To be sure, our bones do ache more with age. But it was Monet, who when crippled with arthritis in his eighties, had the brushes tied to his hands. His vision was clear. It was only his body that was deteriorating. Or if sight goes. as did Georgia O'Keefe's, you can turn from painting to pottery.

Many of the 44 artists in the Elders of the Tribe were in their young-old years and in interviews with them, talked, on the one hand, of an awareness of being older, of being the sum of all the experiences of life till then and, on the other hand, of being the same adult person who has always tried to set up visual problems and solve them. They usually added that they will remain this way as long as they remain healthy. Massos Daphnis in his late seventies put it: "Creating, that's what keeps you young. You're always young when you create. Fortunately, I'm in good health. How much I do today I could have done at thirty." Then when asked what he tells young artists, he says: "Do not try to be a star at thirty. You have to be mature. You have to have experiences to know yourself. All we paint is who we are." Some say, as did the great Japanese woodcutter Hokusai when on his death bed at 94, that they are now only beginning to learn their craft. Estaban Vincente in his mid-eighties said: "I'm still searching: 'Til I die. One thing I will not do is die of boredom."

Whereas most persons of advanced age accept death with equanimity, artists may do as the middle aged Dylan Thomas admonished; that is, not go gently into the night but rather "rage against the dying of the light." Apparently, Picasso did so in drawing inspired pornography at the end of his long life. Still, there are many active and creative very old persons who seem to face the end of their life with equanimity. George Burns on his ninety first birthday, after telling reporters that he will play cards in the afternoon and date a pretty girl in the evening, added in whimsical equanimity: "I have made old age popular. Now everyone wants to be old."

Knowing the Essence

While retaining their creativity, old visual artists invariably talk about seeking, or knowing, the essence of what they wish to portray. They typically say that they have stripped away the superfluous and now can get at the essence or the core or the pure expression of their visual pursuit. Beatrice Wood, the ceramic potter, said at 93, "I am somewhat detached from the need to express myself which I had once." Knowing herself, and with the knowledge that she is still the same person that she had always been, there is a lessening of introspection and a lessened need to discover herself. This is the self-wisdom of the very old. Wood continues: "I don't think about my age. I am happier now. It's only the outer covering that ages. The essence or the soul or whatever is the person never ages. I know I'm over ninety but inside I'm still sixteen or seventeen. I know a lot, but little of the universe. . . . It is a blessing to be 90. You know what is right or wrong. You don't waste time." Expressing the essence of oneself or getting at the essence of one's art is a common theme. The sculptor Peter Agostini, for example, says: "All I am looking for is to get at the essence. In other words I am only looking for essence." Sally Michels the painter puts it: "When you're older you want to say what you want to say." Unlike the young who she says "want to jump on the band wagon."

Classical Composers

Collaboration for focusing on the essence of one's work comes from Simonton's (1989) study of the last works of 172 classical composers. He found that last works, as compared to earlier works, what he called "career swan songs," were "brief, relatively simple in melodic structure, but profound enough to acquire a lasting place in the concert hall" (p. 45). The less emotionality that Simonton inferred was interpreted by him to be an expression of resignation or even contentment as death approached. A different interpretation, consistent with statements by the visual artists, is that the movement toward concise and simplified versions of earlier works reflects the successful capturing by composers of the essence of their earlier works. And, in turn, this capturing the essence of what they wish to express in sound does not tell us that death has become acceptable to them. It does, however, tell us that the self has been preserved.

Preservation of the Self

It is indeed the preservation of the self that is the adaptative challenge in the latter years. Creative individuals who continue to be creative appear to share psychological mechanisms with others of advanced age in preserving the self. Differences do exist, as they do among all individuals. How death is confronted surely differs among individuals, as is how the preservation of self is experienced.

Yet, apparently, very old people are generally able to preserve their identities and in doing so, can maintain feelings of well-being. Possibly, the most successful aging includes not only a preservation of self, encompassing a self-wisdom regarding how that the self is preserved despite age-associated assaults, but also wisdom about the regularities of human existence. This wisdom about human existence, consisted with the conventional definition of wisdom, was apparently characteristic of elderly men in simpler societies. Elderly men joined the culture of the ages, identifying with the gods and feeling powerful in doing so, and were able to be used by all generations to explain the regularities of human existence (e.g., Gutmann, 1987). Without the role of wise elders, wisdom in its truest sense is less encouraged because it is less functional for society and the continuity of generations. Moreover, it is not essential for self-wisdom and the preservation of the self and well-being.

To believe that true wisdom is essential for well-being in the later years is to ignore how the average person maintains his or her sense of a persistent self when becoming "old." Feeling that a personally meaningful life has been lived, often limited to being a member of one's own immediate family, is sufficient for well-being if still mobile and, also, not in crisis. Most significant is to feel that one's life work has been completed, which most people do feel. Creative artists may be an exception, as well as others who still have "unfinished business."

IMPLICATIONS FOR PRACTICE

The emphasis here has been on differences between the old and the young. Yet there may be more similarities than differences regarding issues in the process of dying and acceptance of death and, in turn, how to facilitate an acceptable death. Being in control, without pain and with others are obviously important regardless of age. The stages postulated by Kubler-Ross may be equally inapplicable, or equally applicable, for younger individuals as for older individuals. Personality characteristics, will contribute to differences in acceptance of dying among the young and the old. Preservation of the self until the last breath is important regardless of age, and, also, "unfinished business" can be paramount regardless of age.

Indeed, the middle-aged terminal cancer victim may be able to arrive at a state of acceptance and equanimity by feeling like those persons who feel "old." That is, he or she may feel, often through our assistance, that the life that has been lived, albeit foreshortened, has been meaningful, fully lived and that little or no "unfinished business" is being left behind. The person, on the other hand, who considers him or herself to now have become "old," may, as discussed previously, feel cheated of life as many younger persons do because of "unfinished business."

Yet for those who now experience themselves as "old," the psychological context is decidedly different. Their life course has been lived, and most do perceive and accept that this is so. Acceptance of death can generally come easier than for younger people. Unfortunately, again regardless of age, when dying occurs in a foreign environment such as in a hospital or in a nursing home, especially dying without the presence of family members, it may be quite difficult to accept one's personal death with any degree of resignation and equanimity. Mitigating against the effect of foreign environments on those of advanced age, is the control inherent in making living wills and assigning durable powers to attorneys. Such steps at earlier ages can provide assurance that life will not be sustained if there is not quality to life nor if there cannot be a meaningful quality to life with any of the known therapeutic interventions.

When I Wish to Die

Still, passive euthanasia when personhood appears lost should not be undertaken without appropriate deliberation. Too often older persons espouse hopelessness and wishes to die when, however, reestablishing a sense of self sameness, of one's identity, can reverse this attitude. Moreover, even comatose patients can recover if provided with stimulation, as was illustrated in Chapter 5, on iatrogenesis, by Miss Coons who at 86 was comatose in the hospital for five months. Because of the persistence of her coma, her sister, age 83, implored her sister's physician and lawyer to remove her gastric feeding tube and finally to let her sister die a natural death. A judge agreed. Nursing staff, however, feared that other patients would perceive them as also letting them die and when the gastric tube was removed, began to feed and bathe Miss Coons. Also other patients began to provide attention to Miss Coons.

Apparently, the attention, the skin contact she lacked for several months, helped to revive her as she slowly came out of her coma. Unless we attempt to humanize our care and to reestablish a sense of personhood, we should not assume that an irreversible state with no quality to life is present.

Regarding letting people die, Goldfarb (1983) has written in an edited book entitled *The Right to Die*:

> If our beliefs that a person be allowed to die should he request it (however extensive our review) or that we can let him die (after adequate review of the details) are based upon giving him greater freedom to live and enjoy life as an individual, they would seem acceptable. However, there appears at present to be a glamorization of dying and of being dead which is part of a movement toward enjoining people to savor dying and to welcome death. Dying, we are told, must be dealt with like any other loss, which we first deny, than deal with by stages of anger, bargaining, and finally acceptance. It is acceptance of death, then as early as possible that we should learn? Or should we learn to treasure life so much that the passage through its later stages is fully lived when we see death near? (p. 18)

Understanding Meanings of Death

From another perspective, all human beings must develop their own meanings of both life and death. For the person now "old," meanings will likely be a complex and interacting blend of how the past, present and future are perceived. The past, as part of the "unique psychology of the very old," is actively incorporated into the present, the here-and-now, definition of the self; and also made vivid to preserve the "here-and-now" sense of self. Indeed this normative process of making the past vivid to preserve the self is, as was noted in Chapter 2, the basis of Grunes' (1982) therapeutic approach to the restoration of the self among the very old who are in acute crisis.

Yet the present, too, has its meaning, meanings which are inseparable from those that are provoked from reflections on the past, especially when having "unfinished business" from unfulfilled responsibilities and life goals. When the meanings of the present circumstances of death are dysfunctional for accepting death, including "unfinished business" from situational determinants, death becomes less acceptable and can indeed cause previously latent anxiety to be experienced as manifest or even acutely experienced anxiety or panic and can, also, disorganize a previously cohesive and coherent reconstruction of a self-preserving vivid past.

It is the meaning of the future after death that can be particularly disturbing for those who do not believe in an afterlife that assures a reunion with deceased loved ones. Without this belief, there is no personal future. If, however, death is perceived as a relief from a painful existence or barren life, it can be accepted even without a belief in a personal future after death. When not perceived as a relief, and without a belief in a personal future after death, denial of the reality of non-being can be reinforced by promoting a sense of being the same person throughout the process of dying. Also non-being can be accepted without denial if the meanings of life at the end of life are organized around perceptions of a meaningful life having been lived. That human beings can do so reflects the essence and resolution of our existential paradox. Indeed, we may lose ourselves as we are now but our life course can be perceived as having been lived and having been lived as we were raised to live it. In making life meaningful at death because life has been lived as it should have been lived, transcendence of death becomes possible. It is this kind of transcendence that some would conceptualize as spiritual, as unique to humans and to the human spirit (see, for example, LeFevre & LeFevre, 1981).

Obviously, I have not attempted to be prescriptive but, rather, I have attempted to identify barriers to the acceptance of death at the end of life that practitioners must consider in providing terminal care. Additionally, however, I have attempted to identify possibilities when facilitating the most acceptable death for each individual at the end of life.

FUTURE OF ACCEPTING DEATH

Will we see a change in the future? Although we have increased the length of the relatively vigorous younger old years, as well as the age at which people experience being "old," it may be increasingly difficult to accept one's death. Members of future less religious cohorts, for example, may not perceive themselves to be personally blessed for having lived through their 90s and 100s, and even approaching 110 to 115 years, which is the lifespan for human beings. Given, additionally, more educated future cohorts, it is possible that many will experience life as creative persons do and wish to continue to achieve self-assigned life goals at very advanced ages.

We must, however, be cautious not to glamorize the deaths of exceptional persons such as Hokusai. Whereas Saunders and Kubler-Ross may have done us a great service in drawing our attention to the needs of the dying, there has also come a tendency to romanticize death. Kastenbaum (1982) has discussed the "image of terminal actualization" that requires "the terminal phase of life to be . . . exalted, fulfilling . . . something special, well beyond the dimensions of ordinary experiences" (p. 164). In turn, Shneidman (1971) has urged that death and dying be "deromanticized." Although we may be able to cope with death and dying, in no way do I consider it to be a transcendental experience.

Given beliefs that transcendental experiences are unlikely, we can, however, go the other way and be too receptive to letting elderly persons do away with themselves. To control one's fate is indeed important. Living wills, designated powers of attorney and DNR directives are essential. Yet too easily we can respect wishes to die when restoring the self and hopefulness is indeed possible. Recently, for example, I was asked to consult on a hospitalized patient who had attempted suicide. She continued to talk of suicide to which the geriatric staff responded by an openness to letting people control their own lives. It was apparent to me, however, that her words were hollow. She had reestablished her sense of self, a sense of control and a sense of hopefulness by establishing a relationship with a male aide, reaffirming and preserving her identity as a cherished female.

Even, however, with vigorous efforts to assist elderly people in preserving their identities, as well as in facilitating the acceptance of an acceptable death, it may be less possible to do so in the future. The conditions under which death will occur for future cohorts of the elderly may be more difficult. If, for example, the three leading causes of death were to be conquered (stroke, cardiovascular disease and cancer), we will add years to life but we will also add years that contain irreversible musculoskeletal degeneration with more bedboundness and more Alzheimer's disease. Above 90 years of age, it is estimated, that one of three persons will have Alzheimer's disease! To die with pain and feeling alone, as well as without control because of cognitive deterioration, may be increasingly common; and as we are witnessing, greater numbers may wish to avoid a protracted process of dying. Our task then, as it is now, will be to assure the best possible death, a death in which identity is preserved until the last moments of life and in which death is acceptable because there is no "unfinished business."

Chapter **8**

Final Comment on Practice, Research, and Theory

The content of this book, hopefully, reflects the interaction among practice wisdom, research findings and theory. As noted in the Preface, ideas that emerged from clinical work became hypotheses to be confirmed by studies; and, in turn, hypotheses generated by empirical investigations became hunches to be verified by practice. It is this kind of interaction that provides for phenomena that are too readily misunderstood when in only one world.

CORRECTING DISTORTIONS

One example of a misinterpretation by researchers that has been corrected by practitioners is the reason for the association between more family visiting and lower morale among older people. When large-scale studies of elderly persons revealed this association, some researchers interpreted the finding as reflecting how more intergenerational contact can lead to family conflict, followed by a lessening of older peoples' feelings of well-being. A logical practice implication is to discourage intergenerational contact. "Nonsense!," said practitioners, "your data simply shows that more family visiting occurs when older members are ill and need attention and care. The lower morale comes from being ill and not from family contact!"

A distortion the other way, by practitioners that has been corrected by researchers, is that older people are more clinically depressed than younger people. Anyone who works in long-term care obviously comes in contact with depressed older people. Epidemiological data, however, are incontestable. If anything, there is less clinical depression among the old than among the young.

Correcting distortions is neither easy for practitioners nor researchers. We all become invested in our interpretations of phenomena, and even the most flexible among us find it difficult to relinquish these investments. Yet we must! If we are aware, however, of these rigidities, we can counteract them by avoiding premature closure. Working back and forth from data to their meanings, as well as from research findings and practice wisdom, before the solidification of interpretations, is most beneficial for generating viable theoretical formulations.

AVOIDING PREMATURE CLOSURE

The importance of aggressiveness in reducing advance outcomes to crises among elderly persons is illustrative of the importance of avoiding premature closure. Turner (1969), in her doctoral dissertation, showed aggressiveness to be associated with positive outcomes in one of our four studies of relocation, the Last Home for the Aged study (see Tobin & Lieberman, 1976). Her hypothesis, which was substantiated, was that aggressiveness predicted positive outcomes because this trait was congruent with adaptive demands of the institutional environment. To be sure, congruence between personality traits and environmental demands is an explanation for positive outcomes to relocation. But had we stopped there, we would have missed the saliency of aggressiveness. That is, when the two studies that followed also revealed that aggressiveness was associated with positive outcomes, we were sufficiently open to develop a next hypothesis regarding the role of aggression in facilitating adaptation to relocation and then to crises in general. In turn, returning to the literature provided assurance that the converse of aggressiveness, passivity, was associated with adverse outcomes in extreme situations.

USING PRACTICE WISDOM

Facilitating the broadening of the generalization from the more restricted congruence hypothesis to the more general hypothesis was Grunes' (1962, personal communication) insightful clinical observation imparted to me before the relocation studies that passive men are likely to be in great jeopardy when relocated to Drexel Home for the Aged. Thus, practice wisdom in this instance was of critical importance in understanding results from empirical studies.

Practice wisdom was also helpful for understanding the importance of magical coping for older persons when under stress. Goldfarb, as noted in Chapter 2, had based his brief treatment of residents of the Hebrew Home and Hospital in New York City on inflating beliefs in mastery. His therapeutic approach was indeed congruent with findings of how the transforming of the relocation situation by magical kinds of coping facilitates adaptation.

TOWARD THEORY

A more torturous course, however, was necessary to establish the normative, and beneficial, use of the past for the preservation of the self. Initially, the reconstruction of the past was to be used to predict outcomes to relocation; that is, it was assumed that those elderly persons who had coped best in the past, as reflected in their reconstructions of the past, would adapt better to relocation. Concurrently, however, there was an awareness from our psychotherapy with younger individuals that such reconstructions reveal aspects of current life, including the nature of the transference relationships. Substantiating the latter perspective were scales developed to assess variability in reconstruction of earliest memories that revealed how the level of narcissistic loss in these memories was associated with the meanings of current situations (Tobin & Etigson, 1968). During the preadmission period, while awaiting relocation from the community to nursing homes, for example, themes of abandonment dominated; and after institutionalization, there was a shift to themes of personal injury and illness, as well as of death and dying. At the same time we were influenced by Butler's (1963) formulation of the life review, and we began to assess variability in reconstruction of past life that were gathered in an open-ended format of three hours or so. The working hypothesis was that those whose reviews of their past lives contained a resolution of conflicts would adapt better to the relocation to nursing home.

Although Gorney's (1968) investigation did not reveal this association, he serendipitously found that introspection was inversely correlated with age among our older respondents. Apparently, with aging among these older persons, there is a lessening of introspection.

Then, fortuitously, Revere returned to graduate school to complete her doctoral dissertation after many years as a clinician. Her immersion in the life-review protocols, with much productive obsessing about the reconstructions of the past, led her to design a study to compare the reconstructions of our elderly respondents to the reconstructions of middle-aged respondents. Revere (1971) included among her variables, dramatization of persons from the past, which led to the important finding that older persons are more likely than younger persons to dramatize and make vivid persons from their past as they reconstruct their lives.

When her finding was added to Rosner's (1958), regarding how the past is used interchangeably with the present to define the self in the present, it became possible for Lieberman and me to begin to formulate the unique psychology of the very old. Obviously, the path to our formulation included a willingness to avoid premature closure, but most essential was the receptivity to the interplay between empirical findings from our studies and insights by astute clinicians.

Most Recent Phase

The journey was, however, not yet completed. Only more recently, when I assigned my students the task of interviewing individuals 80 years of age and over living independently in the community, did two critical elements emerge: the importance of the threshold from only being "older" or "elderly" to being "old," and the significance of religious belief in an afterlife.

"Why," I have often asked myself, "did these pieces of the puzzle escape me?" Although a primary focus of my research has been on how older persons adapt to stress, a persistent interest in normative aging dates back to my graduate school years when I worked with Bernice Neugarten and Robert Havighurst on data from the Kansas City Study of Adult Lives. Then, I now believe, I was too single-minded in attempting to disprove Cumming and Henry's (1961) disengagement theory to allow myself to fully listen to what respondents were telling us. Moreover, although the Kansas City interviews provided rich data, there was too little time allotted for respondents to tell their own stories.

It was different for the students who became fascinated with personhood in advanced old age. For them, it was a relief to talk to "normal" people when the rest of their energies were devoted primarily to counseling individuals with psychopathology. Rather than only spending the less than two hours that was necessary to gather the essential data to write up their case study, they began conversations that often lasted more than three hours and even made return visits.

As they presented their case studies in class, lively discussions ensued. I recall the student who became intrigued with the octogenarian who told her that she was "not old yet" because she could still take care of her horses. Although this proud horse woman no longer rode because of a hip replacement, as long as she could be with her horses, she would not consider herself to be "old." As other students added to the animated discussion, I became increasingly aware of the importance of the concept of oldness. Only through their rather lengthy conversations with older persons who were not in crises, followed by the sharing of these conversations with the class, did this element of personhood emerge.

The meaningfulness of religious beliefs, however, was not so unknown to me. My work on the church as service provider, with James Ellor and Susan Anderson-Ray, led me to understand the feeling of being personally blessed by God when living a long life. Yet, the importance of beliefs in an afterlife containing reunions with deceased loved ones had escaped me, most likely because of my own disbelief. Apparently, because of this disbelief, my respondents, as well as clients, were discouraged from discussing private thoughts about an afterlife. The students, who were primarily from working class backgrounds, however, were usually raised to believe in an afterlife and therefore found it natural for their respondents to discuss the topic. Thus, the students' beliefs permitted their respondents to openly reveal the most private of religious beliefs. One student humorously told the class about the widow who had a shrine for her dead dog Rufus and who would stroke his leash when lonely. Yet, the student did not find it humorous that her respondent was looking forward to seeing Rufus again after she died. This anticipated reunion was perceived by the student as natural as the pasta her matriarchical Italian grandmother made almost every day and as natural as her grandmother's daily prayers for innumerable family members who had gone to heaven to reap their devine rewards.

Once again, interacting with non-researchers, this time with novice clinicians in their second year of graduate training for their MSW degrees, was helpful, if not essential.

The many excursions that have been detailed, including the excursions into understanding the acceptance of death at the end of life, have consumed decades of time and effort. Possibly, it is my longevity as a researcher and practitioner that has not only provided me with the necessary maturity to understand the very old but, also, to begin to understand how psychological processes among them transcend their cohort differences.

FUTURE OF PERSONHOOD

When I began my work in gerontology, people in their eighties were born in the 1870s, whereas now they are born after the turn of the century. These two cohorts have had very different early life experiences from differences in the historical times in which they were born, got married, reared children and so forth. Yet the psychological processes of those who have become "old" seems to transcend historical times. However, because the narcissistic assaults of advanced age are occurring later, the qualities of personhood of the "old" that were likely to have been characteristic of those in their seventies 30 years ago are now likely to occur in the eighties or even nineties; and can be expected to occur at even later ages in the future. Unless there are profound changes, it can be expected that the distinguishing qualities of personhood will persist.

Yet, if there are profound changes in socialization and life styles, variants of the unique psychology may emerge to be dominant such as the psychology that is now more characteristic of creative persons; there may be, as discussed in the previous chapter, less acceptance of death. Parallel reasoning also may apply to the androgynous shift in the middle years. It is my impression that when Gutmann began his studies of normative aging over 30 years ago, the androgynous shift in which women are confronted with their aggressiveness and men with their passivity after the postparental imperative was rather graphically evident in his data. Thirty years later, with child rearing becoming more androgynous, the shift in the middle years may not be as dramatic. Will personhood also be different in the future? If so, it will be comparable to conversion hysteria which was common in the 19th Century but has been displaced by existential crises and Alzheimer's Disease.

The changing nature of age-associated assaults may eventuate in parceling out the older years into several developmental epochs. Morris and Bass (1988) have referred to those in their younger old years as "tomorrow's able elderly." After the younger-old years, there may be a phase of near-frail years; followed by the early-older-old years and then the later-older-old years; and next the preterminal years, those marked by immobility from musculoskeletal degeneration and intractable confusion from Alzheimer's disease. If these developmental periods are sensible it can be expected that they would follow in sequence but not be aligned with chronological age as tightly as the developmental periods of the earliest years. If there is anything that we have learned it is the great variability in aging. With age, people do indeed become more different from each other, which includes remarkable differences among people in timing of life events. Regardless of any precise timing, if these developmental epochs are to be meaningful, each should be associated with a somewhat different psychological experience of self. Lacking, however, are systematic studies of how the inner experience of aging changes during the latter half of life.

UNDERSTANDING HUMAN EXPERIENCE

It is indeed necessary to seek to understand the common inner experiences of developmental epochs for cohorts, so that practice can be modified and goals appropriate to developmental epochs be adopted in our work with individuals, families, in institutions and in other settings. This challenge is best accomplished by moving back and forth from clinical experiences to findings from research efforts. Moreover, from listening to, and working with, aging individuals, it becomes possible to not only develop a therapeutic optimism but also an optimism regarding our own future.

Yet studying inner experiences is always arduous. Indeed it is far easier to measure the obvious. But unless, for example, the experience of death is studied in-depth during the phase of terminal drop, little clarity can be provided to practitioners regarding how practice with elderly dying individuals can, and should, be modified. Moreover, researchers must know that distance from death is a variable that can obfuscate findings, for affects as well as for cognitive functioning. But most germane to the treatise of this book is the necessity to investigate through longitudinal studies the transition from being "older" or "elderly" to becoming "old." Our insights into the unique psychology of the "old" emerged from longitudinal studies of relocation. Although systematic, in-depth longitudinal studies of lives are warranted, unfortunately, they tend not to be funded in the current climate of "scientific" inquiry.

If, in turn, findings from studies, as well as practice wisdom, are to be useful, it is mandatory that speculations, models and theories be developed that permit the organizing and synthesis of diverse ways of understanding aging. Surely, hypotheses can be generated followed by attempts at theory-building. In turn, theories should be modified as practice reveals new insights and research negates previous findings. Still, it is vital that theorizing occurs, as was done when developing a way of organizing and synthesizing diverse findings to formulate personhood in advanced old age. Hopefully, therefore, the qualities of personhood will be modified by practice wisdom and research findings and, if warranted, discarded as newly accrued knowledge is synthesized.

Need for Innovative Studies

We must, however, be more innovative in our investigations of human experiences. As social scientists, we have too often been tethered to seemingly rigorous research methods most appropriate to the basic sciences. In 1988, I wrote the following in my farewell editorial as Editor-in-Chief of *The Gerontologist*:

> Given the journal's premier status in gerontology, I am often asked: Where is the field going? I may be able to tell you where it has been, which comes from reading over 1600 submitted manuscripts in four years, but I cannot forecast where it is going. The flow of manuscripts, however, suggests a healthy trend toward investigating the causes for relationships that have been revealed by previous research. Because these investigations sometimes are based on small nonrepresentative samples using other than standardized instruments, they too often are misperceived as unrigorous and unyielding of believable findings. Yet, conversely, too many seemingly impeccable studies, replete with large representative samples and the best of standardized instruments, as well as the latest of statistical analyses, have been rejected by our superb referees. Generating new knowledge depends less upon elaborate designs, state-of-the-art instruments, and sophisticated statistics than upon investigators' capacities to conceptualize researchable problems using the yield from previous studies and the wisdom from practice, openness to select the most appropriate methods for inquiries, and talents to translate findings into their implications for theory, further research and practice. When these attributes are manifested in a manuscript even in the absence of "scientific rigor," referees are quick to respond with favorable reviews. (p. 726)

In-Depth Studies of Meanings

I followed those comments by extolling Karp's (1988) lead article in which he documented the commonalities of aging consciousness among a group of seventy two professional men and women between fifty and sixty years of age. His qualitative, in-depth studies of these peoples' lives revealed how the frequency and intensity of aging messages increases in the fifties, fostering "a quickened sense of aging during this decade." He discussed four general categories of age reminders characteristic of the fifties: body, generational, contextual, and mortality reminders. And he concluded, "The findings reflect a contrast to uniform invariant, and universal stages to adult life. Rather, the contextual events giving rise to distinctive aging consciousness are correlated with age, but not determined by age" (p. 727).

Indeed it is not age *per se* that causes a "quickened sense of aging." Age itself is an "empty variable," as Bernice Neugarten taught me decades ago. Rather it is the meanings of these middle years events that provide the "quickened sense of aging." Similarly, it is the events and their meanings that provoke the experience of being "old" in the advanced years of life. Only, therefore, through studying the meaning of events can the human experiences of different developmental epochs become intelligible.

Human Science Approach

Cohler (1988) rightly has called for a human science approach to understanding meaning, as well as the maintenance of coherence, across the lifespan. His perspective brings social scientists interested in meanings closer to those in the humanities, specifically to those who are interested in the study of subjectivity (like Habermas 1968; 1983; Polkinghorne, 1983; 1988; Ricoeur 1971; 1979; Toulmin, 1979; 1982). Yet, as stated by Cole (1988), "We are just beginning to see scholarly attention to old people as centers of meaning and value" (p. ix). It seems so. Witness the current work of the medical anthropologist Johnson who is interviewing the "oldest old" to "understand the meanings these survivors assign to their lives" (1989, personal communication). Johnson considers her respondents to be "off-time" in living beyond their expectations, which is one aspect of the self-perception of "becoming old." For Johnson, the transition to what I have labelled "becoming old," is associated with a process of "reframing of experience," encompassing new meanings of time, of relationships often characterized by a sense of "aloneness," and the coming to terms with death.

Unless, like Johnson, we focus scholarly attention on meanings associated with developmental epochs, an understanding of, and appreciation for, the human experience in the latter half of life will escape us. Thus we must go further than integrating social science, research and clinical practice wisdom, as reflected in this book, to encompass the diversity of humanistic science perspectives. Only then can we develop the necessary theoretical perspectives for understanding shared human experiences in the developmental epochs in later life.

References

Abraham, K. (1927). The applicability of psychoanalytic treatment to patients at an advanced age. In *Selected papers of Karl Abraham*. London: Hogarth Press.

Antonovsky, A. (1979). *Health, stress and coping*. San Francisco: Jossey-Bass.

Atchley, R. C., (1971). Retirement and leisure participation: Continuity or crisis? *The Gerontologist, 11*, 13–17.

Atchley, R. C. (1989). A continuity theory of normal aging. *The Gerontologist, 29*, 183–190.

Bakan, D. (1966). *The duality of human existence*. Chicago: Rand McNally.

Beauchamp, T. L., & McCullough, L. B. (1984). *Medical ethics: the moral responsibilities of physicians*. Englewood Cliffs, NJ: Prentice Hall.

Becker, E. (1973). *The denial of death*. New York: The Free Press.

Berezin, M. (1987). Reflections on psychotherapy with the elderly. In J. Sadovoy & M. Leszcz (Eds.), *Treating the elderly with psychotherapy: the scope for change on later life*. Madison, CT: International Universities Press, Inc.

Blazer, D., Hughes, D., & George, L. (1987). The epidemiology of depression in an elderly community population. *The Gerontologist, 27*, 281–287.

Brody, E. M. (1985). Parent care as a normative stress. *The Gerontologist, 25*, 19–29.

Brody, E. M., Kleban, M. H., Lawton, M. P., & Silverman, H. A. (1971). Excess disabilities of mentally impaired aged: Impact of individualized treatment. *The Gerontologist, 11*, 124–133.

Bumagin, V. E., & Hirn, K. E. (1979). *Aging is a family affair*. New York: Crowell.

Burnside, I. M. (1981). *Nursing and the aged*. New York: McGraw-Hill.

Butler, R. N. (1963). The life review: An interpretation of reminiscence in the aged. *Psychiatry, 26*, 63–76.

Callahan, D. C. (1987). *Setting limits*. New York: Simon & Shuster.

Callopy, B. J. (1988). Autonomy in long term care: Some crucial distinctions. *The Gerontologist, 28*(Suppl.), 10–17.

Campbell, A., Converse, P., & Rodgers, W. (Eds.) (1976). *The quality of American life*. New York: Russell Sage Foundation.

Carlson, L. (1981). Studies in script theory: I. Adult analogs of a child nuclear scene. *Journal of Personality and Social Psychology, 40*, 501–510.

Childress, J. (1982). *Who should decide? Paternalism in health care*. New York: Oxford University Press.

Cicero, (44 B.C.) (1982) Cato the elder on old age. In M. Grant (translator) *Cicero: selected works* (pp. 214–215). Harmondsworth, England: Penguin Books.

Coe, R. M. (1987). Communication and medical care outcomes: analysis of conversations between doctors and elderly patients. In R. A. Ward & S. S. Tobin (Eds.), *Health in aging: sociological issues and policy directions*. New York: Springer Publishing Company.

Cohen, D., & Eisdorfer, C. (1986). *The loss of self*. New York: Norton.

Cohler, B. J. (1982). Adult developmental psychology and reconstruction in psychoanalysis. In S. I. Greenspan & G. H. Pollock (Eds.), *The course of life, vol. III*. Washington, DC: NIMH.

Cohler, B. J. (1988). The human studies and life history: the social service review lecture. *Social Service Review, 62*, 552–575.

Cole, T. (1988). Introduction. In D. Polisar, L. Wygart, T. Cole, & C. Perdomo (Eds.), *Where do we come from: What are we? Where are we going? An annotated bibliography of aging and the humanities*. Washington, DC: The Gerontological Society of America.

Cooper, K. L., & Gutmann, D. L. (1987). Gender identity and ego mastery style in middle-aged, pre- and post-empty nest women. *The Gerontologist, 27*, 347–352.

Costa, P. T., & McCrea, R. (1984). *Emerging lives. Enduring dispositions*. Waltham, MA: Little, Brown and Company.

Csikszentmihalyi, M., & Rochberg-Halton, E. (1981). *The meaning of things: domestic symbols and the self*. Cambridge, MA: Cambridge University Press.

Cumming, E. M., & Henry, W. E. (1961). *Growing old: the process of disengagement*. New York: Basic Books.

Datan, N., Hughes, F., & Rodeheaver, D. (1988). Life span development. In M. R. Rogenzweig (Ed.), *Annual review of psychology*. Palo Alto, CA: Annual Reviews, Inc.

Diggory, J., & Rothman, D. Z. (1961). Values destroyed by death. *Journal of Abnormal and Social Psychology, 30*, 11–17.

Dobrof, R. (1983). *Training workshops on caring for the mentally impaired elderly*. New York: The Brookdale Center on Aging of Hunter College.

Eaton, M., Mitchell-Bonair, I. L., & Friedman, E. (1986). The effect of touch on nutritional intake of chronic organic brain syndrome patients. *Journal of Gerontology, 41*, 611–616.

Edelson, J. S., & Lyons, W. (1985). *Institutional care of the mentally impaired elderly*. New York: Van Nostrand Reinhold Company.

Erikson, E. H., (1950). *Childhood and society*. New York: W. W. Norton.

Erikson, E. H. (1982). *The life cycle completed*. New York: Norton.

Feifel, H. (1977). Death in contemporary America. In H. Feifel (Ed.), *Meanings of death*. New York: McGraw-Hill.

Fisseni, H. J. (1985). Perceived unchangeability of life and some biographical correlates. In J. M. A. Munnichs, P. Mussen, E. Olbrich, and P. G. Coleman (Eds.). *Life span and change in a gerontological perspective*. New York: Academic Press.

Gallup, G., Jr., & Castelli, J. (1989). *The peoples' religion*. New York: Macmillan.

Gibson, R. C. (1986). *Blacks in an aging society*. New York: The Carnegie Corporation.

Gillick, M., Serrell, N., & Gillick, L. (1982). Adverse consequences of hospitalization in the elderly. *Social Science and Medicine, 16*, 1033–1038.

Goffman, E. (1961). *Asylums*. Chicago: Anchor Books Company.

Goldfarb, A. I. (1959). Minor maladjustments in the aged. In S. Arieti (Ed.), *American handbook of psychiatry, vol. I*. New York: Basic Books.

Goldfarb, A. I. (1983). The preoccupation of society with death and dying. In Group for the Advancement of Psychiatry, *The right to die: decisions and decision-makers*. New York: Jason Aronson.

Gorney, J. (1968). Experience and age: patterns of reminiscence among the elderly (dissertation). Chicago: University of Chicago.

Gould, R. L. (1978). *Transformations: growth and change in adult life*. New York: Simon and Shuster.

Gray, R., & Moberg, D. O. (1977). *The church and the older person*. Grand Rapids, MI: Erdman's.

Grunes, J. M. (1982). Reminiscence, regression and empathy—a psychotherapeutic approach to the impaired elderly. In S. I. Greenspan & G. H. Pollock (Eds.), *The course of life, vol. III*. Washington, DC: NIMH.

Grunes, J. (1987). The aged in psychotherapy: psychodynamic contribution to the treatment process. In J. Sadovoy & M. Leszcz (Eds.), *Treating the elderly with psychotherapy: the scope for change in later life*. Madison, CT: International Universities Press, Inc.

Gurland, J. J., Deen, L., Cross, P., & Golden, R. (1980). The epidemiology of depression and dementia in the elderly: the use of multiple indicators of these conditions. In J. O. Cole and J. E. Barrett (Eds.), *Psychotherapy of the aged*. New York: Raven Press.

Gutmann, D. (1964). An exploration of ego configurations in middle and later life. In B. L. Neugarten (Ed.), *Personality and later life*. New York: Atherton.

Gutmann, D. (1987). *Reclaimed powers: toward a new psychology of men and women in later life*. New York: Basic Books.

Haan, N. (1976). . . . Change and sameness . . . reconsidered. *International Journal of Aging and Human Development, 7*, 59–66.

Haan, N., & Day, D. (1974). A longitudinal study of change and sameness in personality development: adolescence to later adulthood. *International Journal of Aging and Human Development, 5*, 11–40.

Habermas, J. (1968/1971). *Knowledge and human interests*. Boston: Beacon Press.

Habermas, J. (1983). Interpretive social science vs. hermeticism. In N. Haan, R. Bellah, P. Rabinow, & W. Sullivan (Eds.), *Social science as moral inquiry* (pp. 251–270). New York: Columbia University Press.

Handel, A. (1984). Perceived change of self among adults: a conspectus. Paper presented at the International Conference of Self and Identity, Cardiff Wales.

Harris, L. et al. (1975). *The myth and reality of aging in america*. Washington, DC: National Council on the Aging.

Hasselkus, B. R. (1988). Meaning in family caregiving: perspectives on caregiving/professional relationships. *The Gerontologist, 28,* 686–691.

Havinghurst, R., & Albrecht, R. (1953). *Older people.* New York: Longmans Green.

Heisel, M. A., & Faulkner, A. O. (1982). Religiosity in an older black population. *The Gerontologist, 22,* 354–358.

Hofland, B. F. (1988). Autonomy in long term care: Background issues and a programmatic response. *The Gerontologist, 28*(Suppl.), 3–9.

Jahnigen, D. Hannon, C., Laxson, L., LaForce, F. M. (1982). Iatrogenic disease in hospitalized elderly veterans. *Journal of the American Geriatrics Society, 30,* 360–369.

Jahoda, M. (1958). *Current concepts of positive mental health.* New York: Basic Books.

James. W. (1892). *Psychology: the briefer course.* New York: Henry Holt.

Kamptner, N. L. (1989). Personal possessions and their meanings in old age. In S. Spacapan & S. Oskamp (Eds.), *The social psychology of aging. The Claremont Symposium on Applied Social Psychology.* Newbury Park, CA: Sage Publications.

Kane, R. L., Ouslander, J. G., & Abrass, I. B. (1989). *Essentials of clinical medicine* 2nd ed. New York: McGraw Hill.

Karp, D. A. (1985). A decade of reminders: changing age consciousness between fifty and sixty years old. *The Gerontologist, 28,* 727–738.

Kastenbaum, R. (1966). On the meaning of time in later life. *Journal of Genetic Psychology, 109,* 2–25.

Kastenbaum, R., & Candy, S. (1973). The four percent fallacy: a methodological and empirical critique of extended care facility population statistics. *International Journal of Aging and Human Development, 4,* 15–21.

Kastenbaum, R., & Costa, P. T. (1977). Psychological perspectives on death. In M. R. Rosenzweig and L. W. Porters (Eds.), *Annual review of psychology, vol. 28* (pp. 225–250). Palo Alto, CA: Stanford University Press.

Kaufman, S. R. (1987). *The ageless self: sources of meaning in late life.* Madison, WI: University of Wisconsin Press.

Kierkegaard, S. (1844/1957). *The concept of dread.* Translated by Walter Lourie. Princeton, NJ: Princeton University Press.

Kleban, M. H., Brody, E. M., & Lawton, M. P. (1971). Personality traits in the mentally impaired aged and their relationship to improvements in current functioning. *The Gerontologist, 11,* 134–140.

Kleemeier, R. W. (1961, September). Intellectual changes in the senium, or death and the I.Q. Presidential address to Division 20 of the American Psychological Association, New York.

Koenig, H. G., Kvale, J. N., & Ferrel, C. (1988). Religion and well-being in later life. *The Gerontologist, 28,* 18–28.

Koenig, H. G., George, L. K., & Siegler, I. C. (1988). The use of religion and other emotion-regulating coping strategies among older adults. *The Gerontologist, 28,* 303–310.

Komrad, M. S. (1983). A defense of medical paternalism: maximizing patient autonomy. *Journal of Medical Ethics, 9*, 38–44.

Kulys, R., & Tobin, S. S. (1980). Older people and their responsible others. *Social work, 25*, 138–145.

Kuypers, J. (1967). Elderly persons enroute to institutions: a study of changing perceptions of self and interpersonal relations [dissertation]. Chicago: University of Chicago.

Labouvie-Vief, G. (1985). Intelligence and cognition. In J. E. Birren and K. W. Schaie (Eds.), *The psychology of aging*. 2nd ed. New York: Van Nostrand Reinhold.

Langer, E. J. (1989). *Mindfulness*. New York: Addison-Wesley.

Langer, E., & Rodin, J. (1976). The effects of choice and enhanced personal responsibility for the aged: a field experiment in an institutional setting. *Journal of Personality and Social Psychology, 34*, 191–198.

Leary, T. (1957). *Interpersonal diagnosis of personality*. New York: Ronald Press.

Lebowitz, B. D., Light, E., & Baily F. (1987). Mental health center services for the elderly: the impact of coordination with area agencies on aging. *The Gerontologist, 27*, 699–702.

LeFevre, P. (1984). Toward a theology of aging. *The Chicago Theology Seminary Register, 74*, 1–12.

Levinson, D., Darrow, C., Klein, E., Levinson, M., & McKee, B. (1978). *The seasons of a man's life*. New York: Knopf.

Lieberman, M. A., & Tobin, S. S. *The experience of old age: stress, coping and survival*. New York: Basic Books.

Lieberman, M. A., & Lakin, M. (1963). On becoming an institutionalized person. In R. H. Williams, C. Tibbitts, & W. Donahue, (Eds.). *Process of aging Vol. 1: social and psychological perspectives* (pp. 475–503). New York: Atherton Press.

Lindsley, O. R. (1964). Geriatric behavioral prosthetics. In R. Kastenbaum (Ed.), *New thoughts on old age*. New York: Springer Publishing Company.

Lyons, W. (1982). Coping with cognitive impairment: some family dynamics and helping roles. *Journal of Gerontological Social Work, 4*, 3–21.

Mace, N. C., & Robins, P. V. (1981). *The 36-hour day*. Baltimore: Johns Hopkins Press.

Mallya, A., & Fitz, D. (1987). A psychogeriatric rehabilitation program in long term care facilities. *The Gerontologist, 27*, 747–751.

Marchio-Greenfield, E. (1986). C-O-N-N-E-C-T (Communication Need Not Ever Cease Totally): a communication enrichment project for families at the Jewish Home and Hospital for Aged, Unpublished paper.

Markides, K. S. (1983). Aging, religiosity and adjustment: a longitudinal analysis. *Journal of Gerontology, 5*, 621–625.

Marshall, V. W. (1980). *Last chapters: a sociology of aging and dying*. Monterey, CA: Brooks/Cole.

McGrowder-Linn, R., & Bhatt, A. (1988). A wanderer's lounge program for nursing home residents with Alzheimer's disease. *The Gerontologist, 28*, 607–609.

Mead, G. H. (1934). *Mind, self and society*. Chicago: University of Chicago Press.

Miller, M. B. (1975). Iatrogenic and nurisgenic effects of prolonged immobilization of the ill aged. *Journal of the American Geriatrics Society, 23,* 360–369.

Mischel, W. (1969). Continuity and change in personality. *American Psychologist, 24,* 1012–1018.

Morris, R., & Bass, S. (1988). *Retirement reconsidered: economic and social roles for older persons*. New York: Springer.

Munnichs, J. M. (1966). Old age and finitude: a contribution to psychogerontology. *Bibliotheca Vita Humana, 4.*

Myers, W. A. (1984). *Dynamic therapy of the older patient*. New York: Jason Aronson.

Nemiroff, R. A., & Colarusso, C. (Eds.). (1985). *The race against time: Psychotherapy and psychoanalysis in the second half of life*. New York: Plenum.

Neugarten, B. L. (1974). Age groups in American society and the risk of the young-old. In Eis, F. (Ed.), *Political consequences of aging*. Philadelphia: American Academy of Political and Social Sciences.

Neugarten, B. L. (1977). Personality and aging. In J. E. Birren & K. W. Schaie (Eds.), *Handbook of the psychology of aging*. New York: Van Nostrand Reinhold.

Neugarten, B. L., & Datan, N. (1973). Sociological perspectives on the life cycle. In P. B. Baltes & K. W. Schaie (Eds.), *Life span developmental psychology: personality and socialization*. New York: Academic Press.

Neugarten, B. L., & Datan, N. (1974). The middle years. In S. Arieti (Ed.), *American handbook of psychiatry*. New York: Basic Books.

Neugarten, B. L., Havinghurst, R. J., & Tobin, S. S. (1961). The measurement of life satisfaction. *Journal of Gerontology, 16,* 134–143.

Neugarten, B., Havinghurst, R., & Tobin, S. S. (1968). Personality and patterns of aging. In Neugarten (Ed.), *Middle aged and aging: a reader in social psychology*. Chicago: The University of Chicago Press.

Palmore, E. (1980). The social factors in aging. In E. Busse & D. Blazer (Eds.), *Handbook of geriatric psychiatry*. Van Nostrand Reinhold. New York.

Parkes, C. M. (1972). *Bereavement*. New York: International Universities Press.

Perlin, S., & Butler, R. N. (1963). Psychiatric aspects of adaptation to the aging experience. In J. E. Birren, R. N. Butler, S. W. Greenhouse, L. Sokoloff, & M. R. Yarrow (Eds.), *Human aging: a biological and behavioral study*. Washington, DC: NIMH.

Pincus, M. A. (1968). Toward a conceptual framework for studying institutional environments in homes for the aged [dissertation]. Madison, WI: University of Wisconsin.

Pinkston, E M., Levitt, J. L., Green, G. R., Linsk, N. L., & Rzepnicki, T. L. (1982). *Effective social work practice*. San Francisco: Jossey-Bass.

Poggi, R. G., & Berland, D. I. (1985). The therapists' reactions to the elderly elderly. *The Gerontologist, 25,* 508–513.

Polkinghorne, D. (1983). *Methodology for the human services: systems of inquiry*. Albany, NY: State University of New York Press.

Polinghorne, D. (1988). *Narrative knowing and the human services.* Albany, NY: State University of New York Press.

Pollock, G. H. (1987). The mourning-liberation process: ideas on the inner life of the older adult. In J. Sadovoy & M. Leszcz (Eds.), *Treating the elderly with psychotherapy: the scope for change in later life.* Madison, CT: International Universities press.

Revere, V. F. (1971). The remembered past: its reconstruction at different life stages [dissertation]. Chicago: University of Chicago.

Revere, V., & Tobin, S. S. (1980/81). Myth and reality: the older person's relationship to his past. *International Journal of Aging and Human Development, 12,* 15–26.

Ricoeur, P. (1971). The model of the text: meaningful action considered as text. *Social Research, 38,* 529–562.

Ricoeur, P. (1989/81). The function of narrative. In J. B. Thompson (Ed.), *Paul Ricoeur: hermeneutice and the human sciences.* Cambridge, Cambridge University Press.

Riley, M. W., & Foner, A. (1968). *Aging and society.* New York: Russell Sage Foundation.

Robert Wood Johnson Foundation (1989). *Interfaith volunteer caregivers: a special report.* Princeton, NJ: Robert Wood Johnson Foundation.

Rodin, J., & Langer, E. (1977). Long-term effects of a control-relevant intervention with the institutionalized aged. *Journal of Personality and Social Psychology, 35,* 897–902.

Rosenberg, M. (1979). *Conceiving the self.* New York: Basic Books.

Rosin, A. J., & Boyd, M. B. (1966). Complications of illness in geriatric patients in hospital. *Journal of Chronic Diseases, 19,* 307–313.

Roslaniec, A., & Fitzpatrick, J. J. (1979). Changes in mental status in older adults with four days of hospitalization. *Research in Nursing & Health, 2,* 177–187.

Rosner, A. (1968). Stress and maintenance of self-concept in the aged [dissertation]. Chicago: University of Chicago.

Safford, I. (1980). A program for families of the mentally impaired elderly. *The Gerontologist, 20,* 3–11.

Saunders, C. (1963). The treatment of intractable pain of terminal cancer. *Proceedings of the Royal Society of Medicine, 56,* 191–197.

Schlesinger, M. R., Tobin, S. S., & Kulys, R. (1981). The responsible child and parental well-being. *Journal of Gerontological Social Work, 3,* 3–16.

Sherman, E., & Newman, E. (1977/78). The meaning of cherished possessions for the elderly. *Journal of Aging and Human Development, 8,* 181–192.

Shneidman, E. S. (1973). *Deaths of man.* New York: Quadrangle/New York Times.

Shomaker, (1987). Problematic behavior and the Alzheimer patient: retrospection as a method of understanding and counseling. *The Gerontologist, 27,* 370–375.

Simmons, L. W. (1945). *The role of the aged in primitive society.* New Haven, CT: Yale University Press.

Simonton, D. K. (1989). The swan-song phenomenon: last works effects of 172 classical composers. *Psychology and Aging, 4,* 42–47.

Smith, G. C., & Tobin, S. S. (1989). Permanency planning among older parents of adults with lifelong disabilities. *Journal of Gerontological Social Work, 14,* 35–59.

Smith, K. F., & Bengtson, V. L. (1979). Positive consequences of institutionalization: solidarity between elderly parents and their middle-aged children. *The Gerontologist, 19,* 438–447.

Snyder, L. H., Rupprecht, P., Pyrek, J., Brekhus, S., & Moss, T. (1978). Wandering. *The Gerontologist, 18,* 372–80.

Snyder, R. (1981). Religious meaning in the latter third of life. *Religious Education, 76,* 534.

Steele, K. (1984). Iatrogenic disease on a medical service. *Journal of the American Geriatrics Society, 32,* 445–449.

Steele, K., Gertman, P. M., Crescenzi, C., & Anderson, J. (1981). Iatrogenic illness on a general medical service at a university hospital. *The New England Journal of Medicine, 304,* 638–642.

Steinitz, L. Y. (1980). The church within the network of social services to the elderly: case study of Laketown [dissertation]. Chicago: University of Chicago.

Suls, J., & Mullen, B. (1982). From the cradle to the grave: comparison and self-evaluation across the life-span. In J. Suls (Ed.)., *Psychological perspectives on the self, vol. I.* Hillside, NJ: Lawrence Erlbaum Associates.

Swann, W. B., Jr. (1983) Self verification: bringing social reality into harmony with the self. In J. Suls & A. G. Greenwald (Eds.), *Psychological perspectives on the self, vol. 2.* Hillsdale, NJ: Lawrence Erlbaum Associates.

Taylor, S. E. (1989). *Positive illusions: creative self-deceptions and the healthy mind.* New York: Basic Books.

Taylor, R. J. (1986). Religious participation among elderly blacks. *The Gerontologist, 26,* 630–636.

Taylor, R. J., & Chatters, L. M. (1956). Church-based informal support among elderly blacks. *The Gerontologist, 26,* 637–642.

Tobin, S. S. (1988). Editorial. *The Gerontologist, 28,* 725–726.

Tobin, S. S., Ellor, J. W., & Anderson-Ray, S. (1986). *Enabling the elderly: religious institutions within the service system.* Albany, NY: State University of New York Press.

Tobin, S. S., & Etigson, E. C. (1968). Effects of stress on the earliest memory. *Archives of General Psychiatry, 19,* 435–444.

Tobin, S. S., & Gustafson, J. (1987). What do we do differently with elderly clients? *Journal of Gerontological Social Work, 6,* 29–46.

Tobin, S. S., & Lieberman, M. A. (1976). *Last home for the aged: critical implications of institutionalization.* San Francisco: Jossey-Bass.

Tomkins, S. S. (1986). Script theory. In J. G. Aronoff (Ed.), *The structuring of personality: the Murray lecture.*

Toulmin, S. (1979). The inwardness of mental life. *Critical Inquiry, 6,* 1–16.

Toulmin, S. (1982). The construal of reality: criticism in modern and post-modern science, *Critical Inquiry, 9,* 93–111.

Turner, B. F. (1969). Psychological prediction to adaptation to the stress of institutionalization in the aged [dissertation]. Chicago: University of Chicago.

Turner, B. F., Tobin, S. S., & Lieberman, M. A. (1972). Personality traits as predictors of institutional adaptation among the aged. *Journal of Gerontology, 27,* 61–68.

Vaillant, G. E. (Ed.). (1977). *Adaptation to life.* Boston: Little, Brown.

Veatch, R. (1981). *A theory of medical ethics.* New York: Basic Books.

Wacker, R. (1985). The good die younger: does combativeness help the old survive? *Science 85, 6,* 64–68.

Weinberg, J. (1974). What do I say to my mother when I have nothing to say? *Geriatrics, 29,* 155–159.

Weissert, W. G. (1985). Estimating the long-term care population: prevalence rates and selected characteristics. *Health Care Financing Review, 6,* 83–91.

Yalom, I. (1987). Foreword. In Sadavoy, I., & Leszcz, M. (Eds.), *Treating the elderly with psychotherapy: the scope for change in later life.* Madison, CT: International Universities Press.

Zarit, S. H., Orr, N. K., & Zarit, J. M. (1985). *The hidden victims of Alzheimer's disease.* New York: New York University Press.

Zinberg, N. E., & Kaufman, I. (1963). Cultural and personality factors associated with aging. In N. E. Zinberg & I. Kaufman (Eds.), *Normal psychology of the aging process.* New York: International Universities Press.

Index